Wm Bates

GESTALT PSYCHOLOGY

Its Nature and Significance

DAVID KATZ, Ph.D.

PROFESSOR OF PSYCHOLOGY
THE UNIVERSITY OF STOCKHOLM

Translated By

ROBERT TYSON, Ph.D.

DEPARTMENT OF PSYCHOLOGY AND PHILOSOPHY
HUNTER COLLEGE

THE RONALD PRESS COMPANY ⋅ NEW YORK

To the memory of my
brother, William.

PREFACE TO FIRST GERMAN EDITION

My association with Gestalt psychology is of long standing; the decision to write this book on the subject is recent.

In 1913, when Kurt Koffka appraised my book on color phenomena, he expressed the opinion that the investigations reported in it would influence all psychological research. I would like to think that Koffka also had in mind the theory which I advanced to explain perception of illumination. Actually it was the first theory of illumination which emphasized holism rather than atomism. The volume on color appeared in 1911, a year before Wertheimer published the work in which he expounded a theory of visual perception of movement based on holism.

In 1925 I published *Der Aufbau der Tastwelt* [1] which broke away completely from the atomistic views of the tactile sense which had prevailed until then. A decidedly holistic emphasis is found, too, in the research on conversation analysis which I carried out with my wife in *Conversations with Children* (1936). And, to conclude the list, the nucleus of my *Hunger und Appetit* [2] (1932) is a theory which embodies the principle of dynamic self-regulation of the organism, so vital for Gestalt psychology.

Although I have always applied the Gestalt viewpoint in the investigations mentioned, and in others as well, there was nevertheless no occasion for evaluating the Gestalt principles themselves. That will be the purpose of this book. In spite of the fact that my views are close to those of the Gestalt psychologists in many, perhaps even in most respects, I do not agree with them completely. I do not believe that all psychological facts are in accord with the Gestalt viewpoint. Personalistic psychology, too, has pointed out the limitations of Gestalt psychology. The purpose of my critical comments is to continue the discussion of Gestalt psychology.

---

[1] *The Structuring of Touch Impressions.*
[2] *Hunger and Appetite.*

A Swedish translation of this book has been published by the Cooperative Press, Stockholm.

DAVID KATZ

Stockholm, August, 1943

PREFACE TO SECOND GERMAN EDITION

The second edition is substantially revised and enlarged. The additions are due, almost without exception, to the results of an experimental approach to new problems from the Gestalt viewpoint. I have in mind primarily the new chapters on Gestalt laws governing mental work and the transposition of action forms. Here, too, the fruitfulness of the Gestalt approach has been demonstrated.

In the meantime a second edition of this book has appeared in Swedish, and translations into Spanish, French, Finnish, and Italian are either completed or in preparation.

Stockholm, March, 1948

PREFACE TO AMERICAN EDITION

This book made its first appearance, in 1942, in Swedish. Since then editions in German, Finnish, French, Italian, and Spanish have been published or are in preparation.

The volume is not restricted to a critical presentation of those aspects of Gestalt psychology which seem significant to me. Rather, in addition it offers results of an experimental approach to new problems from the Gestalt viewpoint. I have in mind primarily the chapters on Gestalt laws governing mental work, the phenomena I have termed "connective inhibition" and "mental dazzle" as they appear in thought processes, and the transposition of action forms. Here, too, the fruitfulness of the Gestalt approach has been demonstrated.

The incentive for this English edition originated with Professor C. A. Mace, of Birkbeck College, London, and Dr. Robert Tyson, of Hunter College, New York. The latter carried out the translation from the second German edition, and I wish to express my sincerest appreciation for his work.

With this book I send cordial greetings to my friends in the Anglo-Saxon countries.

DAVID KATZ

Stockholm, May, 1949

CONTENTS

x   CONTENTS

GESTALT PSYCHOLOGY

CHAPTER 1

ATOMISTIC PSYCHOLOGY AND GESTALT PSYCHOLOGY

According to Hegel scientific knowledge advances in the triple rhythm of thesis, antithesis, and synthesis. The rise of Gestalt psychology can be understood only as a reaction to so-called atomistic psychology. Will it eventually arrive at a synthesis with the doctrine it still attacks, as might be anticipated according to Hegel? The leading Gestalt psychologists find this unthinkable. What they would not deny is that one can hardly explain the essence of the psychology they champion without reference to atomistic psychology. This cannot be contested. Therefore several cardinal points on which Gestalt psychology opposes the older psychology will be presented here.

The older psychology, now condemned to death, is blamed not only for being atomistic. In describing it the publications of leading Gestalt psychologists also make use of such expressions as "associationist," "positivistic," "summative-aggregative," "mosaic-like," "additive," "piecemeal," "mechanistic," and "mechanical." Each of these characterizations is supposed to hit upon a weakness of the older psychology. In addition, atomistic psychology is blamed for having been unrealistic, spiritless, blind, meaningless, and senseless.

One wonders if a scientific psychology with such monstrous attributes could exist even for a short time. The answer is that the accusers are guilty of a certain exaggeration and have produced a caricature of the older psychology rather than an accurate portrayal of it. That this psychology had its shortcomings is undeniable. Perhaps, in observing that its critics have overshot the mark, one could find an ameliorating circumstance by agreeing with Goethe that a person despises no faults as inten-

sively as those he has himself thrown off. For all the leading
Gestalt psychologists once followed in the tracks of the older
psychology before they discovered the path to the only true, new
"form" of psychology.

What is atomistic psychology? Atomistic thinking goes back
to Greek materialism, whose world consisted of minute elements,
indivisible, endowed with specific energies. This view has tri-
umphed particularly in the natural sciences, above all in chemistry. From the natural sciences atomistic thinking was trans-
mitted to physiology. The organism was represented as a combination of the smallest elements, namely cells; if one could
achieve insight into the function of the single cell, comprehension of the work of the whole organism would come about automatically, to a certain extent, by summation.

The reflex was assumed to be the basic element of organic
movement. In the organism isolable pieces of reflex apparatus
of constant build and constant response were said to react col-
lectively on environmental events. Reflexes either facilitated or
inhibited each other. What actually happened in the organism
resulted from addition and subtraction of these individual oper-
ations. It was Pavlov whose reflexology carried this view to its
most extreme formulation.

The reflex concept was taken over by the older psychology to
serve its needs. It had the advantage of being mechanical; in an
organism controlled exclusively by reflexes events take place as
if in a machine, albeit a very complicated one.

Most researchers who have paved the way for modern psychology came from the natural sciences. It is easy to understand how they assumed the atomistic outlook at the same time
that they took over the experimental method from the natural
sciences. The experimental method acquitted itself so splendidly
in the new area that its right to operate there has never been
questioned. The Gestalt psychologists, too, may be counted
among its warmest adherents. But critical deliberation revealed
that an atomistic approach to the nature of mental life could not,
or at least could not by itself, do justice to the task.

By no means did an atomistic approach require only reflexological thinking. There was more to it than that. By preference

the interest of the founders of experimental psychology turned first to sensation. To this day, in fact, the study of sensation has remained one of the most important borderlands between the natural sciences and physiology and psychology. And precisely there, in the field of sensation, the atomistic viewpoint seemed to justify itself fully on the basis of the anatomy of the sense organs and particularly through the discovery of the punctiform sense organs of the skin. Individual cutaneous sense spots were realities to which one could cling; their isolated stimulation corresponded to the individual sensations themselves, the "atoms" of sensory experience.

If in dealing with environmental objects—as opposed to isolated stimulation of single sense spots in the laboratory—whole groups of cutaneous sense spots were activated, it was apparently nothing more than a "summative-aggregative" phenomenon. This concept applied to other sense modalities as well. Several million cones and still more millions of rods are located in the retina. Although it is impossible to stimulate only one of these millions of individual organs, proper experimental technique enables one to excite a segregated few with the result that a point of light is perceived. If a larger surface is seen, that merely indicates that many of these points of light have been combined. It is an exclusively "space-summative" process. The resulting sense impressions actually arose in an additive manner from separate sensory elements.

The process described seemed quite obvious and the explanation of its origin seemed entirely satisfactory from the natural science standpoint. The experiment permitted artificial dissection and reconstruction of the natural sensory process. There was a clear analogy with the analytic and synthetic methods of natural science. This accounts, too, for the expression, "mental chemistry," which had been used occasionally. The appellation, "mental chemistry," becomes particularly clear when the impressions concerned depend on several senses. Take, for example, eating vanilla ice cream. What does mental chemistry have to say about the resulting taste impression? First of all an element of temperature is stipulated, namely an impression of coldness. To this are added the element of sweetness from the taste area, vanilla aroma from the olfactory sphere, and another element, softness, from the sense of touch. If it is desired, the picture can be completed by adding the yellow color mediated by the sense of sight. Thus, according to the older psychology, the result is this simple formula:

Vanilla Ice Cream = Cold + Sweet + Vanilla Aroma + Softness + Yellow.

The older psychology believed it had solved its problem by setting up this sort of formula. But in the ice cream example, as is the case with every disorganized sum total, one can begin or end with a different element without making a vital change. That is what Gestalt psychology means when it speaks of the older psychology as "summative-aggregative," "piecemeal-additive," or "*and*-connected." One element after the other can be dropped from that summative complex, "taste of the ice cream." And with the dropping of the last one, in a positivistic sense, the whole impression dissolves into nothing.

Gestalt psychology cannot come to terms with the outcome to which mental chemistry leads. The whole is more than the sum of its separate parts and not, in the positivistic sense, the sum alone. The basis for that conclusion will be made clear later. For the moment we will pursue the atomistic way of thinking a little further.

Other psychological elements must be considered, in addition to sensations arranged in space and time. First of all there are images, which the older psychology usually described as weaker copies of sensations. And, according to the older psychology, the stream of consciousness makes its appearance as a result of sensations and images which are associated by contiguity in time and space. That is "associationism." Any image could become connected with any other just as a matter of chance.

By means of detailed investigations an attempt was made to provide the concept of the mechanics of imagery—introduced to psychology by Herbart—with a more precise content. Take, for instance, the work (1911–1917) of G. E. Müller, one of the most brilliant exponents of experimental psychology. It was his fixed determination to track down the laws of a pure mechanics of imagery by using materials as devoid of meaning as possible, namely nonsense syllables. Nevertheless, a mechanics of meaningless elements could hardly do justice to the liveliness of meaningful thought and phantasy. It is just this discord in the older psychology which is the target of Gestalt psychology's reproachful designation, "mechanical."

As explained already, sensations and images were said to become associated in space and time. The older psychology solved its space-time problem, as well, in an atomistic manner. We have touched on the question of spatial atomism, as a result of which the impression of extended surfaces arose in a summative manner from the smallest tactile or visual elements. We turn now to atomistic treatment of the time problem, which overshadows the space problem in importance.

Basically the older psychology thought it was possible to effect a sort of atomizing of the stream of consciousness without misrepresenting its structure in so doing. Just as an anatomical preparation is dissected to study its morphology, it was considered feasible to analyze a conscious process into the smallest time fragments to understand its structure. The so-called tachistoscopic method, a favorite of the older psychology, is well suited to this viewpoint. Very brief impressions, perhaps of visual stimuli, are offered possibly for fractions of a second and the phenomena which occur under such conditions are studied. The tachistoscopic method might be called the time miscroscopy of psychology. It is supposed to result in analysis, cleavage, dissection. It is supposed to help trace the adhesion points of sensations and images, the mental atoms, and thus track down the very foundation stones of consciousness itself. Indeed, Gestalt psychology still turns readily to the tachistoscopic method for evidence of form-creating forces; but naturally enough it opposes the time atomism from which the technique arose.

It was time atomism, above all, which prevented the older psychology from recognizing the whole wealth of natural mental forms.

CHAPTER 2

GESTALT CRITIQUE OF OLDER DOCTRINE

Three topics are vital points of reference for a presentation of Gestalt concepts. They are the theory of pure sensation, the constancy hypothesis, and the problem of perceptual constancy.

Gestalt psychology has not always conducted its battle against atomistic psychology with reference to the anatomy of the sense organs. As far as the psychology of perception is concerned, it has far more frequently directed its attack against the theory of pure sensation as expounded in the older psychology.

Before Gestalt psychology applied its critique it was believed that psychology's analysis of sense impressions should be restricted to pure sensation. The purpose was to describe those experiences which are directly connected with stimulation of sense organs, devoid of further interpretation. The manner of approach was so-called introspection. This view can be explained most easily in the field of visual impressions.

Let us say there is a round box before us on a table, and that we look down on it from an oblique angle. If some one asks about the shape of the box we report—if we are unbiased—that the box looks round. Yet the older psychologist would have disputed this statement. Actually, he would point out, we do not see the box as round, but simply interpret the sensory impressions in that way.

The older psychologist would continue in this manner:

The decision that the box was round was possible only because we knew from experience that this was so. Introspection does not give the impression of a round box, but of an oval one. The retinal image of the box is oval because we have a slanting view of it, and the psychologist's task is to see objects as they are represented on the retina.

The older psychologist would explain further that the layman, too, can achieve the impression for which the psychologist strives. For instance, he can hold a net veil between the box and himself, as was occasionally done in art schools to demonstrate the laws of perspective, and imagine the box projected on the surface of the veil. Then he could free himself of his "illusion" and see the box as it actually is represented on the retina, in its oval form. We would be assured that the oval form is the "pure" one, unaffected by higher mental activities.

True, the older psychology would gladly admit that illusion about form interpretation is thoroughly desirable. It provides accurate knowledge of environmental objects. It would be most unfortunate if the shapes of objects changed continually as their inclination to the line of vision changed. After all, the retinal image does change in this way. It would mean the end of proper orientation to the external world. Shapes would no longer be experienced in an orderly fashion, but as chaos. Fortunately the "illusion" about the true form of the retinal image protects us from such an eventuality.

Just how does the older psychology explain the accurate judgment which corrects pure sensation? It goes on to say that pure sensation, the actual retinal image, is altered in the course of experience. Knowledge gained by association with objects is added to sensory impression.

Particular emphasis was placed on the sense of touch. Through contact with objects the touch impressions connected with them would remain the same for a time even if their visual impressions changed continually. The persistence of tactile experience would insure our ascribing a constant shape to the box. It is precisely the round shape that would become symbolic of all the other retinal variations because we would really see the box as round, and coinciding with the retinal image, if it happened to be directly in front of us.

The older psychology concluded that sensations suspected of having an admixture of knowledge gained through experience cannot be regarded as genuine, simple, sensory impressions.

One concept which finds expression in the theory of pure sensation is that which postulates a rigidly fixed correspondence between local stimuli and experience. The oval experience, that is to say, matches the local oval image on the retina. It has become customary to designate this assumption as the constancy hypothesis. In antiatomistic psychology this concept had to yield to one directly opposed to it. According to the contrary view local stimulation does not solely determine the subjective impression it makes and has a surprisingly slight effect on it. Today it is asserted that experience apart from local stimulation depends on the total pattern of excitation of the sense organ concerned, as well as on the stimulus constellation of the other senses. In the last analysis it depends on the condition of the entire organism. Clearly this formulation rejects any fixed correspondence between local stimulus and experience. Moreover, it was advocated before the Gestalt psychologists made use of it in their battle against atomistic psychology.

If the round box preserves its shape independently of the observer's orientation to it, this fact is an example of the constancy phenomenon, or, more precisely, form constancy. It should be noted that the term "constancy hypothesis" as employed in atomistic psychology should not be confused with "constancy phenomenon" in the sense of antiatomistic psychology.

Constancy of form is not the only constancy phenomenon that contributes to interpretation of environmental objects. Constancy of size and color are of particular importance.

The round box may again be of service, this time to illustrate size constancy. It is held directly in front of us and is moved backward and forward. As long as it is not brought too close to the eyes or too far away it always seems to be of approximately the same size. Yet as a linear measurement the size of its retinal image varies enormously in this process, certainly as much as the ratio of 1 to 10. It is obvious that the box does not seem ten times as large when it is near, or one tenth as large when it is more distant. The conclusion is that the apparent size of an object is remarkably independent of the size of the local retinal image.

With different procedure a white box may be used to clarify the concept of color constancy (Katz, 1935). First it is placed in good light near a window and then it is moved to the back of the room where the light is weaker. The amount of light the box reflects may be reduced by as much as 90 per cent. A simple experiment demonstrates the extent of light reduction:

Place the white box at the back of the room and observe it through a small hole in a cardboard shield. The hole should seem completely filled by the surface of the box. Generally a black shield, known as a reduction shield, should be used so that the brightness of the surface appearing in the hole will seem equal to the brightness of the surrounding portion of the shield. By using a black cardboard shield it can be shown that the box at the back of the room reflects surprisingly little light. The color appearing in the hole conveys a true picture of light intensity corresponding to the retinal image, and actually reflected by the "white" box. If the observer then glances again at the box without the reduction shield it looks white, as it did before.

Even an immediately preceding experience with the reduction shield, which gave an accurate view of the objective light intensity of the retinal image, does not influence the color impression of the box seen without the shield. This fact does not speak well for the atomistic concept which emphasizes the importance of experience for correct interpretation of local stimuli. There could hardly be more convincing proof that the impression of an object's color is notably independent of the local stimulus situation.

Form, size, and color constancy are the best known constancy phenomena, but by no means the only ones. Others may be noted briefly.

If an object is moving at a constant speed but is seen from various distances, its apparent speed does not change to any great extent. Perceptual speed constancy is maintained in spite of the fact that the corresponding speeds of the retinal image vary considerably.

Sounds heard from various distances seem to be of approximately equal intensity. This holds true although their objective intensity changes markedly.

Also included among constancy phenomena are touch and kinesthetic experiences which mediate impressions of roughness, smoothness, softness, and elasticity. These interpretations are remarkably independent of the specific sensory activity concerned. The same can be said for perception of weight. Apparent weight of an object changes very little with varying modes of lifting. Lifting it with one or more fingers, a hand or an arm, or even with the teeth, makes the subject change his estimate only slightly.

Finally, reference should be made to the relationship between the sensory constancy phenomena described above and the tendencies which give rise to constant temperature, constant blood pressure, and the constant inverse calcium-sodium ratio in the body fluids. These trends, and others as well, are often included in the term, "wisdom of the body," and justify the view that striving for maintenance of equilibrium is an important characteristic of the organism (Cannon, 1939).

An understanding of Gestalt psychology requires that constancy phenomena be protected from certain misinterpretations which were proposed by the older psychology. The field of color constancy will clarify this need.

An adherent of the older psychology might advance questionable arguments to explain how the white box, although it may at times reflect very little light, is nevertheless seen as white. It is really a matter of inference about a color, he could suggest, rather than a genuine sensory experience. The inference would be based on a thought process such as this: "What I see at the back of the room is dimly illuminated. If I saw it under good illumination I would judge it to be white." Since the thought process would not be completely conscious, it would become necessary to speak of an unconscious inference.

Reference to an unconscious inference is reminiscent of the "illusion" cited previously. But one formulation is as false as the other. It should be emphasized that the color of the box is seen as an immediately present reality in both cases. In both cases it is a matter of genuine color perception and that alone. Whoever denies this might well be asked two questions. Just why is the sight of the box in the dim background not a genuine perceptual experience? Why is it not just as reasonable to say that the impression of whiteness near the window came about through an unconscious inference?

The writer proved many years ago that recognizing the whiteness of the box when dimly illuminated could not possibly depend on previous experience. The most telling part of the proof was the fact that color constancy could be demonstrated even if the object in question had never been seen before. Obviously, then, experience could have played no part in the process.

Some might say that the battle against the doctrine of pure sensation and unconscious inference is a battle against straw men. This is hardly the case. Helmholtz himself advocated the theory of pure sensation. It had the support of Ernst Mach. In contemporary English philosophy it is represented by Bertrand Russell. Helmholtz believed that pure sensations were independent of changes in the observer's attitude. But he overlooked the fact that in every single instance the observer's attitude plays a part even if the perceptions concerned seem "normal." Methods used to demonstrate pure sensations—as in the case of the reducing shield—are after all merely *new* perceptual conditions.

There is no such thing as pure sensation, floating freely in the air, without perceptual conditions. The nonexistence of pure sensations is analogous to the nonexistence in physics of physical occurrences in their own right, without the observer and his attitude. As is well known, this fact is most significant for modern atomic physics.

Since the hypothesis of constant coordination between local excitation and constant impressions appears untenable, a question remains to be answered. What can be said about principles governing the relationship between stimulation of sense organs and conscious phenomena?

At this point the field concept of newer physics may be applied. It is the total visual stimulus pattern which determines the color experience in a certain part of the visual field. When a weight is lifted its evaluation is determined not only by tension in those muscles immediately concerned with the act, but by the tonus of the total remaining musculature as well.

Later pages will show the full significance of the field concept for sensory perception and other areas of psychology.

The next step in the critical survey of the older psychology will be proof that the idea of a rigid, constant relationship between stimulus and experience does not apply even to motor acts. The critique of the atomistic constancy hypothesis for motor phenomena will follow a course similar to that just employed in the field of sensation.

CHAPTER 3

THE PLASTICITY OF MOTOR PROCESSES

Rigid reflexology has been subjected to severe criticism. Goldstein (1934) carries this to the point of questioning the existence of reflexes in the true sense of the word. He points out that the same reflex cannot always be produced in the same part of an animal. He raises a question of fundamental significance by asking how a mere sequence of reflexes could enable an organism to make complex adjustments.

The strongest arguments against atomistic reflexology have come from observation of animals on whom ingenious amputation experiments have been performed (Katz, 1937). Their compensation for such injury is not what would be expected if adaptive movements developed in accordance with the reflex concept. On the contrary, the animal instantly readjusts itself to its customary requirements of spatial movement by using the motor apparatus it still retains. No tedious relearning intervenes.

If one or more of the original six legs of a beetle are cut off, the movements it makes with its remaining legs involve completely new combinations. Even if all the beetle's legs are removed it uses its mandibles for locomotion. Yet these organs have never before functioned in such a manner either in the animal's own lifetime or, it is reasonable to assume, in its entire phylogenetic history.

Amputation experiments with vertebrates have produced similar results. If both hind legs of a dog are removed, as soon as the wounds have healed he walks by swinging the rear part of his body between his front legs. Or he may walk on his front legs and keep the rear part of his body elevated. If his front legs are removed he walks on his hind legs like a kangaroo.

Again the readjustment takes place without the painstaking practice required by the principle of trial and error.

For a considerable period of time the writer had the opportunity of observing a dog which had lost both left legs in an accident. The animal made amazingly skillful use of the two legs on the uninjured right side.

One final example may be cited to demonstrate instant readjustment under extreme circumstances. A guinea pig which is deprived of all four legs tries to move by rolling its body.

Every instance mentioned reveals astonishing plasticity of motor structures. The old theory that a particular motor center with its afferent and efferent neural fibres has a fixed, permanent function must be discarded. It is inconceivable that neural connections conduct stimuli from one part of the central nervous system to another in a rigid and unalterable manner. The amputation experiments prove that what occurs in one motor innervation center has repercussions on all the others. Holism replaces the older atomistic view of the central nervous system.

Magnus (1924) believes that the function of the spinal cord changes somewhat from one moment to the next and thus reflects the changing conditions and locations of various parts of the body and of the body as a whole. According to this view the central nervous system does not determine what occurs at the periphery, but, on the contrary, peripheral events shape the processes of the central nervous system. The old concept of constant motor centers is displaced by the theory that the periphery creates temporary centers in the brain and spinal cord. Some centers develop comparatively slowly. Others, like those concerned with the amputation experiments, come into being suddenly. This formulation is a special case of the principle of organic self-regulation, which will be elaborated upon in later pages.

Motor readjustment is particularly striking in the lower animals mentioned. However, it is by no means lacking in human beings. Righthanded individuals, having learned to write with their right hands, can also write with the left hand without previous practice. If a subject is required to do so he can write with a pencil held with his teeth or with his toes.

Obviously such acts would not have been practiced except under the most unusual conditions.

The writer has conducted many experiments with motor adjustment of war amputees. When an arm is lost there is a surprisingly quick transfer of activity to the other arm. Even when both arms are lost—fortunately a rare occurrence—the amputee can help himself to some extent by using his feet.

It may be noted that when the individual loses his larynx he can express himself fairly well with his remaining speech organs. Burger and Kaiser have reported on this condition. It is not a common situation, but bears on the problem at hand.

The cited examples of motor adaptation by humans lend further support to the principle of dynamic self-regulation of the organism.

CHAPTER 4

THE PHENOMENOLOGICAL METHOD

In psychology an unprejudiced attitude is referred to as *descriptive* or *phenomenological*. For instance, in our discussion of color constancy we rejected the view that judgment of object color was based on illusion or unconscious inference. Instead we appealed to simple, undistorted description of color circumstances as they appeared. The phenomena were allowed to speak for themselves, as it were.

Ewald Hering (1905), the noted physiologist, applied the phenomenological method most profitably in his classical investigations of color vision. A philosopher, Husserl (1901–1902), made systematic use of it and expanded its application. It is no exaggeration to state that comprehension of contemporary psychology necessitates an understanding of the phenomenological method.

Phenomenology has had a particularly profound influence on Gestalt psychology. Indeed, the critique which Gestalt psychology directs against the older psychology, and its own positive contributions as well, stand or fall on the merits of the phenomenological method. It is a serviceable method in all psychological areas. The field of perception can serve as an example.

The effort to describe what actually is present in perception may be hindered by certain errors. One of these is the stimulus error. It consists of confusing knowledge of physical causes with the sensations they produce. Answers to the question, "When do we see the deepest black?" supply illustrations of the stimulus error.

Many subjects reply that the deepest black would be experienced in a completely dark room, one without a trace of light. This appears logical because everyone knows that the impression of brightness increases with stronger illumination. It seems an obvious conclusion that if all light were excluded the result would be absolute blackness. The matter may be extended beyond the abstract reasoning just described, by having subjects actually carry out observation in a totally dark room. A considerable number report that they see absolute blackness, yet their judgment is erroneous. A truly unprejudiced, descriptive attitude reveals that a dark room does not really produce the impression of absolute blackness. The unbiased observer sees a dark gray, which is termed "subjective visual gray." But if the subject adds his *knowledge* of the situation to the dark gray actually present in his perception, he reports on complete blackness. He has fallen victim to the stimulus error.

An impression of deep blackness is not obtained by shutting out all light, but by having a circumscribed, weakly illuminated part of the retina stand out against a strongly contrasting background. The deepest black results from contrast.

Often the stimulus error is associated with what Köhler (1933) termed the "experience error." According to Köhler we "unconsciously and erroneously ascribe certain common characteristics of the visual field to a currently present stimulus constellation because they seem to belong there."

It is obvious that separate, functional, units do not exist as such on the retina. Such local stimuli are associated merely by *"and*-connections." True structuring takes place in higher neural centers.

A problem concerned with perception of space can be clarified by means of the phenomenological method. A study of it supplements the discussion of the stimulus error and supplies further evidence against the older view that all sensations are bound up with local stimuli.

With good illumination the empty space between the observer and the objects around him seems filled with light. Yet it can easily be proved that these apparently bright spaces supply the eye with no light at all, or at most with subliminal quantities of it. Is it possible that we really do not see the empty space as bright, but merely infer that it is bright? The reply is negative, because this phenomenologically faulty conclusion is another example of the stimulus error. There is no doubt that the empty space which seems filled with light is a sensory experience. But its local stimulation cannot be demonstrated to the satisfaction of the older psychology. The apparent brightness of empty space is a so-called covariance phenomenon, and is caused by light impressions of the objects which surround that empty space. The light impressions of those objects, in turn, are determined by the total stimulus pattern of the retina.

It was once the prevailing view of almost all philosophers and other investigators that causality could be comprehended only in the form of abstract imagery. Recently Michotte (1946) was able to furnish proof that causality can in fact be mediated by sensation. He applied the phenomenological method to experimental perceptual situations which were devised with unusual skill. Thus the experience of causality is a primary phenomenon, a highly significant finding.

It was MacLeod (1947) who pointed out that social psychology, "one of the most challenging and one of the least disciplined fields of psychological research," could look forward to rejuvenation and deepening of its concepts as a result of the introduction of the phenomenological method. He effectively indicated that its impact on social psychology would be as significant as it was in the case of the psychology of perception.

Köhler (1933, pages 15–17) has made more extensive use of phenomenology than other Gestalt psychologists. His occasional references to an "experienced table" or an "experienced chair" should be understood in the light of that observational method. Needless to say he does not mean the physical chair or the physical table, but refers to those objects as they appear phenomenologically. At times he places more weight on the data supplied by "naïve" subjects than on that produced by professional psychologists, who may be "prejudiced" observers.

Köhler replies to the accusation that Gestalt psychology has completely renounced analysis, one of the most important aids to scientific research. He states (1933) : "Analysis that yields genuine elements, which actually exist in organization, is a legitimate pursuit of Gestalt psychology. Surely it is more valuable than analysis into pure local sense data which do not even appear as such to the observer." The analytic method recommended by Köhler is definitely based on phenomenology.

CHAPTER 5

THE PSYCHOLOGY OF PERCEPTION

An examination of one of the most representative works in the field, Koffka's *Gestalt Psychology* (1935), shows clearly the question to which it has given the greatest attention. It is the psychology of perception. In terms of pages it accounts for approximately half the book.

No doubt perception is an important concern of scientific psychology. But surely it is not the most important one. It can hardly be said that Freud devoted any considerable interest to perception. This fact may represent a shortcoming of psychoanalysis. On the other hand it also proves that one can make a significant contribution to psychology without taking up perception as intensively as did Koffka.

What accounts for Gestalt psychology's focus on perceptual problems? To begin with, the close association between Gestalt psychology and the physiology of the sense organs forms a vital part of its early history and is still apparent. Since so much of the older psychology dealt with that aspect of behavior, Gestalt psychology had good cause for basing its growth on it. The strength of that early fixation explains why Gestalt psychology has freed itself less completely from sensory ties than might be desirable. It is by no means as easy to understand why Gestalt psychology, in its larger orientation toward perception, has been so preoccupied with visual phenomena. This exaggerated emphasis on vision is demonstrated by the fact that 95 per cent of the pages in Koffka's volume which deal with perception is given over to visual phenomena. However, it cannot be denied that vision serves well as an introduction to Gestalt principles, and the present discussion starts with an example in that area.

Let the reader imagine himself seated at his desk. Before him are a typewriter, writing paper, an inkwell, some books, a pack of cigarettes, matches, and an ashtray. These are strewn about in some disorder. Why is it that each object appears as an independent entity? The layman might consider the question so superfluous that he would take it as further evidence that psychology is the science of useless knowledge. Actually the question is by no means superfluous, particularly when regarded in the light of Gestalt theory.

The question can be restated in several more specific queries: Why is it that the inkwell and ashtray, which happen to be visually contiguous, do not appear as a unit? Since the typewriter partially obscures a pad of paper, why are these objects not seen as one unit? How does it happen that the pile of books is seen as a collection of separate entities, rather than as one whole? Is it because these articles have always been used separately, so that their fixed boundaries have become known? If so, then the ability to perceive would be determined by individual experience.

Gestalt theorists reply that all visual percepts are influenced by knowledge that comes with experience. But experience by no means plays the major role in forming objects into separate entities. Objects constitute themselves for other, more deep-seated reasons, and it is these which account for our ability to have experience with objects in the first place. The distinction is a vital one.

According to Gestalt psychology, as opposed to the older theory, the tendency to form objects would become operative in the consciousness of a child from the start, even without experience of any sort. This would be equally true in the visual field of an individual who was born blind but had undergone a successful ophthalmological operation. In support of its viewpoint Gestalt psychology maintains that we often comprehend objects as units before we have any way of knowing what they are like. This applies to vision in comparative darkness. It occurs in strange surroundings when we come upon objects we have never before seen.

The characteristics of environmental objects have either been given by nature or have been created by human agency. Those created by man usually have more rigidly circumscribed shapes and uniform color which contrasts with the colors of other objects. However, as a rule natural objects such as trees, stones, and water surfaces also stand out in some relief because of sharp contours, common color, similiarity of surface structure, and other factors which indicate common destiny or common origin.

The data presented introduce an important Gestalt hypothesis: that all objects appear as closed units originally, without experience, if they are formed into wholes by the factors mentioned. Detailed verification of this hypothesis is the subject of the following chapter.

CHAPTER 6

GESTALT LAWS

A basic problem for Gestalt psychology is the identification of factors which organize the visual field into independent units. In choosing experimental material for this purpose investigators have shown a preference for figures composed of points and lines. Their example will be followed, but with certain reservations.

There is reason to believe that factors other than those to be outlined play a role in shaping the objects seen in everyday life. It is easy to overestimate the significance of laws illustrated by artificially and ingeniously contrived figures; they are so far removed from the actual environmental conditions to which adjustment must be made. Like optical illusions, point and line figures are instructive and fruitful for Gestalt theory. But how many individuals have ever really fallen victim to an optical illusion in ordinary experience?

Presented below are the six conditions which play an important, if not exclusive, role in producing visual forms:

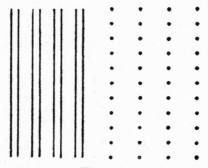

Figure 1

1. *The law of proximity.*

Other things being equal, in a total stimulus situation those elements which are closest to each other tend to form groups.

In Figure 1 the lines closest to each other form pairs, or stripes, separated from each other by the larger spaces. The dots closest to each other are grouped into rows separated by larger spaces.

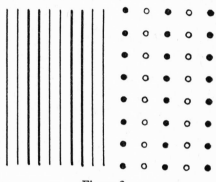

Figure 2

It is possible to see other combinations of the lines and dots. But this requires much greater effort, and succeeds only against distinctly noticeable resistance.

2. *The law of similarity.*

When more than one kind of element is present, those which are similar tend to form groups.

In Figure 2 the heavy lines combine to form pairs. The empty circles are seen in columns, as are the solid disks. In this instance grouping by similarity takes place in spite of the fact that the distances between unlike elements are equal to the distances between similar ones.

Grouping may also occur when only certain parts of elements have similar color or form. An object often appears unitary because all areas of its surface have similar color; this similarity may be due to natural or artificial causes.

3. *The law of closed forms.*

Other things being equal, lines which enclose a surface tend to be seen as a unit.

Triangles, squares, and circles are examples of closed surfaces. In Figure 3a lines 1 and 2, 3 and 4, 5 and 6, etc., combine to form pairs. But in Figure 3b the lines which combine are 2 and 3, 4 and 5, 6 and 7, etc.

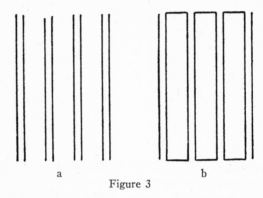

a   b

Figure 3

The law of closed forms plays an important part in organizing the visual field into objects whether they are familiar or unfamiliar.

4. *The law of "good" contour, or common destiny.*

Parts of a figure which have a "good" contour, or common destiny, tend to form units.

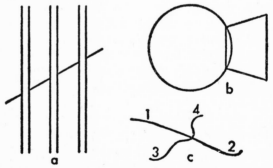

Figure 4

In Figure 4a one sees a straight line which is crossed by pairs of lines. The various parts of the straight line present a good contour and seem to be continuations of each other; they seem to "belong" together. Figure 4b breaks up into a circle and a trapezoid because the parts of each have common destiny and "good" contour. In Figure 4c lines 1 and 2 combine, while 3 and 4 form a separate unit.

In many instances the law of "good" contour and common destiny prevents parts which belong to different objects from combining. It helps one to "see apart" objects which are in visual contact with each other, but which do not have a common destiny and lack "good" contour.

5. *The law of common movement.*

Elements are grouped when they move simultaneously and in a similar manner.

A company of men in marching formation is an example of the law described. By the same token, groups are seen as separate units if they move toward or away from each other.

Two projectors can be used to demonstrate the effectiveness of movement in creating forms. Groups of dots—one group from each projector—are projected onto the same part of a screen, so that they form one haphazard collection, one sum total. However, when one projector is moved the dots projected by it combine immediately and are set apart from the other, motionless, set of dots. As long as motion continues the two groups do not merge. As soon as the moving group comes to a standstill in its former position all the dots again blend into a single chaotic group. Another situation arises when both projectors are moved at the same time but in a different manner. For instance, if one is moved along a straight path and the other along a curved one, two groups of dots are seen simultaneously in the course of separate movements, with the projection screen as a stationary point of reference.

The five laws listed are convincing evidence that environmental objects are seen exactly as they appear at the time of observation. Gestalt psychology maintains that the laws operate even in a consciousness that has had no opportunity to have experience with objects. The assumption, naturally, is that this consciousness has the required degree of maturity. Studies of several blind individuals whose sight was restored confirm the view that visual forms need not depend on experience (Révész, 1938).

6. *The law of experience.*

Comprehension of symbolic forms is partly dependent on the circumstances under which they were learned.

Although it is obvious that Gestalt psychology rejects the dominating role of experience as seen by the associationists, it nevertheless acknowledges the cooperation of experience with the five factors already mentioned. This concession is inevitable. "The nervous system," states Wertheimer (1925), "evolved under the influence of the biological environment; it is only natural that the Gestalt tendencies which developed in the process reflect the orderly conditions of that environment." But Gestalt psychology goes further than acknowledgment of experience in this biogenetic sense. Individual experience, too, shapes our impressions.

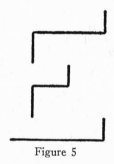

Figure 5

A person who knows the Latin alphabet would regard the three separate lines in Figure 5 as a capital "E." He would report a distinct impression of those contours of the letter which are not objectively present in the drawing. If the figure is rotated in a 90° arc the "E" is no longer seen as distinctly as before. Instead there appear to be three independent lines.

Letters are learned in a specific spatial orientation. When a letter is seen out of its usual orientation recognition becomes more difficult, and the role of experience becomes apparent.

Letters are by no means the only visual phenomena whose recognition depends on a particular spatial position. Whenever lines have a symbolic function, as in words, letters, and diagrams, their comprehension is partly based on orientation in space. It is difficult to read print turned upside down and impossible to read poor handwriting in that position. If a photograph of a person is held upside down his facial expression is unrecogniz-able. Gestalt psychology has only recently concerned itself with problems such as those mentioned. The connection between form comprehension and fixed spatial orientation can be ap-proached in a satisfactory manner only by comparing senses with and without expressive and symbolic aspects. The tactile mo-dality has no expressive aspect whatsoever. It has only a slight symbolic problem, most closely related to the blind.

With the exception of the last law described, those favoring creation of visual forms are all concerned with external condi-tions. For Gestalt psychology individual experience amounts to "consolidation of a natural response of the visual system" (Köhler, 1933). In addition there is said to be a Gestalt tend-ency. It is only natural that inner Gestalt tendencies differ from one individual to another, varying especially with their interests and activities. An artist's training, for instance, consists to a considerable extent of providing him with certain definite form tendencies.

A general, nonindividual, factor that plays a part in determin-ing visual forms is termed "pregnance." The important role ascribed to pregnance requires a preliminary discussion of its background, to be followed by a chapter devoted to the specific topic.

CHAPTER 7

THE SCOPE OF THE GESTALT CONCEPT

Gestalt psychologists have given the form concept an exceedingly wide scope. The following discussion will demonstrate its comprehensive nature.

Vision may again serve as a convenient point of departure, with optical illusions as subject matter.

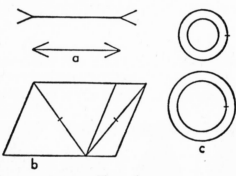

Figure 6

Figure 6 presents three familiar examples of optical illusions. Briefly, the shafts in 6a seem to be of different lengths; one diagonal of 6b seems longer than the other; and the inner circle in the lower portion of 6c appears larger than the outer circle in the upper portion of the diagram. Yet the parts mentioned are equal. Each illusion in Figure 6 depends on the total context in which the particular misjudged parts are placed. Their attributes are influenced by their relationships in that total context.

Optical illusions were a knotty problem for the older psychology because it sought an atomistic explanation for them. Actually they can be understood only from a holistic viewpoint.

The whole illusional figure must be considered; it cannot be viewed as a collection of elements.

Ambiguous figures are other visual forms which must be viewed holistically. In the light of Rubin's basic investigations they are of the greatest interest as examples of the figure-ground relationship. In Figure 7 it is possible to see an upright cross

Figure 7

against a background of circles or a different cross against a background of diagonals. Another ambiguous drawing is shown in Figure 8, which may be seen as a row of black letters "T"

Figure 8

with a white background or a repeated white motif with a black background.

Figure-ground phenomena are of fundamental importance for psychological theory. They can be demonstrated in all sense modalities. But they are particularly distinct in the case of hearing, when a voice or tune is heard in relief against a background of other sounds.

The extent to which the relationship between perceptual elements is transposable has been the subject of numerous Gestalt inquiries. Color forms deserve emphasis in this connection.

Figure 9 shows two pairs of color forms which are the basis for an experiment of a type that has been performed with lower animals and children. An animal may be trained to react to the lighter gray in 9a by having it connected with food. At a later time the animal will react to a darker gray if it is then combined with one still darker, as is the case in 9b. Clearly the animal

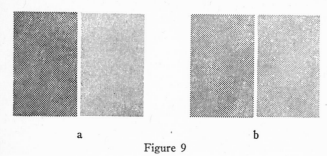

a   b

Figure 9

reacts to the total color form, and the color form is transposable. The animal is said to have endowed the pair of colors with a form quality which is transferred from one color pair to the other. Transposition of form quality reduces atomistic explanations to absurdity.

There are certain conditions of illumination which are almost nonexistent in everyday life, but which can be distinctly significant for Gestalt theory. They involve a clearly circumscribed, comparatively small portion of the visual field whose color remains objectively constant, while the brightness of its surroundings continuously varies. As a result the relative brightness of the two areas would never be the same from one moment to the next. This situation can be arranged in the laboratory, with the purpose of having subjects evaluate the inner area, particularly with respect to its brightness. If judgments of the inner area can be made without great difficulty, and remain essentially constant, there is added evidence that the color form as described in the preceding paragraphs has limited effectiveness. Moreover, the limitations of the Gestalt viewpoint would be demonstrated in a sensory field, an area in which it has been outstandingly influential. It is now possible to report on an investigation by two of the writer's students, Keller and Takemasa (1933), who produced proof that judgment of a circumscribed area remained constant although the surroundings were altered.

Keller and Takemasa made use of a small gray area whose surroundings varied continually from extreme brightness to darkness. Evaluation of the gray area was almost unchanged in these circumstances, and represented practical constancy in different relationships. It is particularly interesting to note that this outcome received behavioristic confirmation in experiments with chickens, the very animals which had served to prove the transposability of color forms. These results refute any claim that constant judgment of a color detached from its surroundings depends on verbal symbolism. Since the findings are so important, and since, to the writer's knowledge, they have never been accorded deserved recognition in Gestalt literature, it seems appropriate to present them as formulated by Keller and Takemasa: "There are circumstances under which a color (a surface color) which is a constituent part of a visual field can accurately be perceived in its own right even when its relationship with the surrounding area changes during the period of presentation. Thus, even under the difficult conditions of our experiments, an objective color can be extricated most effectively from its 'structural' and 'form' bonds with its surroundings" (1933, page 133).

Patterns of movement, whether genuine or apparent movement, should be included in the category of forms mediated by vision. The impossibility of understanding such movements atomistically is just as much a fact as the fact of perception of movement itself.

A distinction should be made between meaningful and meaningless movements. Only expressive movements are meaningful. As a rule they are produced by living creatures, either human or animal. All biologically essential movements are meaningful. They are the ones by means of which humans and animals reveal their friendly or inimical inclinations toward each other.

How does it happen that all breeds of dogs, from the largest to the smallest, with so many variations of appearance, recognize each other as dogs even from a considerable distance? Such recognition must depend on the movement pattern involved. In the case of humans mimicry and pantomine may be added in so far as they are comprehended by another human being.

An example of meaningless movements may be seen in Wertheimer's (1912) phi phenomenon, which has been of such central interest in Gestalt psychology. The phi phenomenon is apparent movement produced by presenting two visual elements

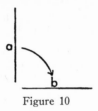

Figure 10

in two different locations, with a short time interval. In Figure 10 lines "a" and "b" represent surfaces which are illuminated in rapid succession, so that "b" follows "a" as a quick sequence of visual events. Under these circumstances apparent movement from "a" to "b" is easily perceptible.

Acoustic forms have had a special place in Gestalt theory. A metronome may be used to demonstrate them.

If the subject hears a series of metronome beats separated by short intervals it is practically impossible to think of each beat as isolated. Two, or several, always combine to form a rhythmic series. The rhythmic effect becomes more distinct if all the beats are not presented at equal intervals, but in such a manner that two or three always follow each other with the same separation, and are separated from the next group by a longer pause. Thus the law of proximity applies to acoustic as well as visual forms.

The law of similarity, already applied to visual figures, also operates in the case of acoustic phenomena. If in a series of metronome beats at equal intervals two loud beats are consistently followed by two soft beats, the soft beats will be grouped and the same may be said for the loud ones. They will be heard as subrhythms in the total rhythmic pattern.

All rhythmic processes, whether they occur in music, danc-ing, or everyday colloquial speech, can be treated scientifically only if regarded from a holistic viewpoint. No rhythmic experi-ence is explainable on an atomistic basis.

The holistic approach is essential for an understanding of why melodies exist. From the time when von Ehrenfels origi-nally established his two Gestalt criteria of melody they have been a mainstay of antiatomistic evidence. Von Ehrenfels first pointed out that a tune cannot be comprehended as a mere sum of its constituent notes, but must possess a particular form quality. The second criterion concerned the transposable nature of a tune. To transpose a tune means to shift it higher or lower. The result may be that the original tune has not one single note in common with the transposed tune. Yet the tune itself is retained. It is the form quality that remains the same when such shifting takes place.

There are other acoustic processes which defy atomistic inter-pretation. For instance, radio reception may be so disturbed by interference—accidental or intentional—that it is difficult to hear the announcer. Noise becomes an acoustic background against which word forms stand out in just enough relief to make the broadcast intelligible. This ability is an amazing audi-tory achievement. Microtomic analysis would arrive at scraps of sound devoid of meaning or expression because it could not regard speech elements as forms against the background of noise elements.

Integration over a period of time makes speech intelligible. If the noisy background is not too loud, a meaningful spoken word can be heard astonishingly well in spite of being relatively soft. But that is by no means the only achievement of which the ears are capable. The auditory sense can do more than separate the forms of two simultaneous acoustic series, one of which is meaningful and the other meaningless. Suppose music and a conversation are added to the radio speech with its background of noise. All are sounded at the same time. Even under those circumstances it is possible to follow and comprehend any one of the four separately organized acoustic series at will. Every attempted atomistic explanation falters in the face of this accomplishment.

All mental processes occur in the course of time. However, this does not mean that the passage of time, as such, always enters consciousness in the same way, or that it must enter consciousness in the first place. An individual can become aware of the passage of time in its various forms of duration, succession, change, or rhythmic organization. In the case of acoustic phenomena these forms may be either more or less intrusive. There are conscious states which run their course in time, but in which time is consumed or altered in the production of other patterns. This may occur in all sense modalities, although the following illustration continues in the auditory field.

Let us say that the subject hears a slight noise and localizes it in space. He places it to the left and nearby. How is such localization accomplished? It depends on a difference in the time at which each ear is stimulated. The difference is astonishingly small, and may be as little as 1/20,000 of a second or perhaps even less. However, it does not enter consciousness as a time difference, but is transformed into an experience of direction. Literally, therefore, time becomes direction, or, in the instance mentioned, a conclusion about space. This is a remarkable dual function of the ear with respect to space and time. It is as if time "stiffens" when direction is localized in space. An atomistic interpretation is utterly insufficient.

When time functions with space it is not completely obliterated as it was in connection with sound. It remains recognizable, either in the focus of attention or phenomenologically sensed in the background. An example of phenomenologically perceived time occurs when a bird is recognized by the way it flies, or a distant human being by his walk.

Observation of animals bears witness that the response to movement is biologically deep-seated. Many animals react only to moving nourishment. Even if they are extremely hungry they ignore their usual food if it is motionless. There are many animals whose copulatory behavior, with its preliminary and sequential acts, is entirely determined by the partner's movements. Nothing reveals the fruitlessness of time atomism as clearly as the biological roots of the strongest drives, hunger and sex. They are firmly planted in time and motion patterns.

Touch is among the sensory areas neglected by Gestalt psychology, although it produces an especially high yield of whole forms. For the most part commentators content themselves by pointing to a very small number of investigations, such as those carried out by Benussi. He discovered, for example, that by touching three triangularly placed spots on the skin he could evoke a circular impression. Or reference may be made to the findings of von Skramlik and others (1937). They proved that the reaction to touch on one part of the skin was affected by stimulation of a neighboring spot.

Gestalt literature fails to make note of the great wealth of tactile forms which have been demonstrated by other investigators. Depending on the arrangement of the stimuli in time and space, the sense of touch responds with experiences of pressure, pull, tickle, itch, and vibration. Still others are roughness and smoothness, hardness and softness, and elasticity. These tactile forms are revealed only in the course of movement. Since they could not be placed adequately in the older psychology, they were granted nothing more than curiosity value.

Are there olfactory forms? They could hardly be forms comparable to structured figures. But the olfactory sense is just as remarkable for its wealth of characteristics as it is for its poverty of structure. It can be the bearer of the strongest emotions, and therefore plays a most important biological role. There is a startling discrepancy between this biological significance and the lack of form mentioned. Perhaps, despite the conviction of Gestalt psychology, there are wholes of higher biological valence which do not fit into the Gestalt system. If smell becomes part of a taste pattern, together with temperature and touch impressions in the oral cavity, it contributes to food forms. Recalling a previous illustration, the vanilla ice cream is by no means an "*and*-connection," but constitutes a form which is more than the sum of its component parts. To date Gestalt psychology has completely neglected gustatory forms. Yet they control hunger, one of our most powerful drives.

Still another example of the Gestalt concept is seen in a sentence. Whether read or heard, it can be experienced as a unit. Even an extensive dialogue can make a unitary impression. The discussion of a problem by a learned society can be experienced as a whole unit by those taking part in the meeting. Consider the detailed proof of a mathematical theorem. If it could not be presented in such a way that its separate but articulated parts remained vivid in consciousness, how could it possibly be understood? Gestalt psychology would regard these examples as thought patterns. They are undoubtedly wholes with the attributes of figure forms.

Gestalt psychology includes action forms in its research realm. These should be divided into instinct, drive, and insight forms.

Emotional patterns are ordinarily dealt with in connection with the psychology of volition, and the same holds true for form problems associated with the self.

Gestalt psychology has not been content with a positive definition of the nature of Gestalt. In addition it has undertaken to prove unsatisfactory those explanations of wholeness which are made without completely abandoning the fundamentals of atomism. The relationship theory and the production theory of forms should have brief consideration.

It has been claimed that a form depends upon comprehension of the relationship between its parts or between the elements of the stimuli producing it. In short, the relationship theory maintains that the form is identical with comprehension of this relationship. Thus a tune would be identical with comprehension of the relationships between its individual notes. Gestalt psychology does not deny that there are both psychological and physical relationships between the notes of a tune and that it is possible to discern them by means of appropriately directed analytical activity. As a result of such analysis it would be observed that the first note of a tune is related to the second, the second to the third, and so on. But would the actual experience of hearing a tune have anything to do with understanding these relationships? Even the notes which do not immediately follow each other are in a specific, fixed, relationship to each other. If it seemed desirable, these additional relationships could be brought to light as well as the ones already referred to. It is only necessary to observe how many of these relationships there are to realize that the original, simple experience of hearing a tune cannot have much to do with the relative position of its notes. The tune is immediately present and offers itself to the listener. But the same cannot be said of the relationships between its notes; these must be *sought*. Clearly the tune form cannot be identical with comprehension of the relative position of its notes. To generalize, a form experience is not identical with comprehension of the relationships of its parts.

With equal determination Gestalt psychology resists the production theory, which views form as a sort of supplementary phenomenon. A tune, for instance, would be a superstructure supported by individual notes. Wertheimer (1925) opposes this position by stating: "Forms are not summations of constituent elements, subjectively built of parts primarily present and possessing only subjectively determined structure."

The best known production theory has been advanced by the Austrian "Graz school." For these theorists the form concept has two strata, the supporting elements and their superstructure of form. Gestalt psychology views form as consisting of only one stratum, since it is thought of as immediately perceived. The argument which can be directed against the production theory is similar to that applied to the relationship theory. It is precisely the immediacy with which form makes its appearance. Activity such as seems indicated by the expression, "production," is not essential for a form experience. We undoubtedly have a certain amount of freedom to analyze a form. But it is an exception, not the rule, when we make use of it.

In the opinion of Gestalt psychologists there is no area of general psychology which does not come within the scope of the form concept. Their dictum goes too far. All forms are wholes, but systematic critique proves that not all wholes are forms. It is most probable that the form concept applies to an intermediate area of undeliberated mental processes. It would therefore be particularly fruitful for genetic psychology.

CHAPTER 8

FORM PREGNANCE

An important law may now be added to the list of Gestalt principles already presented. It is the law of pregnance.

Koffka (1935, page 110) formulated the law of pregnance in these words: "Psychological organization will always be as good as the controlling circumstances permit." It should be emphasized that "good" refers to such characteristics as regularity, symmetry, inclusiveness, unity, harmony, maximal simplicity, and conciseness.

Gestalt psychology considers the pregnance concept to be of the greatest significance. It is universal. It operates in every individual regardless of experience. In more specific terms it means that the organism has a tendency toward certain modes of behavior, whether they are perceptions, movements, or attitudes. The nature of these tendencies will be made clear by a number of examples:

a   b

Figure 11

A number of dots arranged in an approximately circular fashion are seen as if they were on a true imaginary circle. An angle of 87° or 93° looks like a right angle.

Drawings with gaps, such as those in Figure 11a and 11b, tend to be seen as closed.

A figure which is not entirely symmetrical may nevertheless seem symmetrical if the observer does not examine it too closely. And it will be recalled from previous pages that rapid and successive stimulation of three triangularly located spots on the skin produces the impression of a circle.

In each instance mentioned the subject organizes the stimulus situation into an experience as "good" as controlling circumstances will permit. They are examples of the law of pregnance as it applies to pure perception.

The following phenomena are drawn from the sensori-motor field:

The lens of the eye always adjusts itself so that the clearest possible image falls on the retina; the accommodation process comes to a halt only when optimal clarity has been achieved, thus offering a prime example of "good" organization. The older reflex theory of the lens mechanism could not explain accommodation, since precisely the same light stimuli are present before and after optimal accommodation has been established.

The law of pregnance also manifests itself in the process of visual fixation. The eyes adjust themselves to the point where an object that was in the visual periphery is brought into the center of the field. According to Koffka (1935, pages 311–316), fixation of an object represents an equilibrium in the visual field.

Pregnance plays an important part in spatial localization of sound. Adjustment of the head toward the source of sound can be understood only with reference to that law. If the sound is in the median plane of the head the stimulus conditions are as simple as possible, because both ears are stimulated at the same time. Or, if both ears are equally sensitive, they are stimulated with equal intensity. By means of adjustment toward the source of sound a balance of forces in the stimulus-response system is said to have been brought about.

Gestalt psychology attempts to explain imitation with reference to equilibrium. The original model for the imitated movement and the movement itself are regarded as balancing each other. Here reference can be made to a principle formulated by Köhler (1913). He maintained that when we hear a note we are in some measure forced to reproduce it.

Just what is it that causes the organism to act in accordance with the law of pregnance? Scheerer speaks of individual oscillations in the psychophysical organism. Others refer to internal form pressure. In any event, methods have been developed for intensifying the internal factor to make it more easily observable. Four methods are outlined.

1. The tachistoscope may be used. If an irregular figure is exposed for $\frac{1}{10}$ of a second it usually appears more regular. The determining retinal stimuli have a purely evocative function. The individual oscillations of the organism take over the stimulation and convert it to greater regularity. Figure 11, already referred to, can be used for tachistoscopic presentation. Under those circumstances the gaps in the drawings are not seen. The subject reports a closed circle and a closed triangle.

2. The same drawings—shown in Figure 11—can be used to demonstrate internal form pressure. However, the conditions under which they are shown must be varied. They are exposed for an unlimited length of time under very weak illumination. Again a strong tendency toward pregnance appears.

3. An effect similar to that obtained in "1" and "2" above is produced by presenting the same figures reduced in size. Or the same result can be achieved by placing them at a greater distance. If the drawings are then gradually enlarged—or if they are gradually approached—the so-called actual origin (*Aktualgenese*) of the forms can be traced. From preliminary forms their gradual development toward a final, permanent form is seen in progress. As the figures approach their last stable stage the tendency toward pregnance is always obvious. They are organized into the "best" form conditions will permit.

4. The tendency towards pregnance is also clearly revealed in the afterimage. For instance, if afterimages of Figure 11a and 11b are induced, the gaps which objectively exist in them disappear and the figures close.

Tension between the individual oscillations of the psychophysical organism and the demands of the stimulus constellation—as they strive toward equilibrium—occasionally expresses itself in the instability of the subject's impressions. When it is presented tachistoscopically a dot which is not exactly on a circle appears to move toward it.

Taking understandable pleasure in their discovery, Gestalt psychologists have paid particular attention to investigations of pregnance. However, they have often claimed that this phenomenon, and this phenomenon in particular, proves the so-called nonrandom nature of mental connections and hence their original purposefulness. The writer cannot accept this view without reservation.

Sensory pregnance tendencies share their nonrandom nature with other phenomena which were known long ago. Examples are optical illusions and contrast phenomena, which can hardly be said to be purposeful. Is it purposeful if the subject sees that which is not circular as circular, a right angle where there actually is an angle of 87° or 93°, or does not see a gap which has objective reality? In these and other similar situations the pregnance tendency leads to error, and certainly that end cannot be described as having a purpose. In sensation the pregnance tendency is conducive to misperception rather than perception. Only by overcoming it do we arrive at an accurate evaluation of the environment.

A different view of the pregnance tendency may be advanced. It is a structural disposition of the organism which had to be taken as part of the whole organic "bargain" because of certain advantages which were tied up with it. The reference here is to optical illusions and contrast phenomena. These had to be included because of the way in which the eye is constructed. The contrast phenomenon is incidental to an adjustment which is advantageous in its own right, namely reciprocal action of elements in the field of vision. It was Hering who offered this description (1905), maintaining that every element of the retina strives to produce a complementary process in every neighboring element.

Contrast phenomena do not interfere seriously with orientation to the environment. Optical illusions are of even less practical significance. As indicated in another connection, they are usually introduced in the laboratory under artificial conditions.

It would not appear justifiable to claim that all sensory processes which follow the law of pregnance are purposeful.

Assertions about the operation of pregnance in the sensorimotor area remain to be discussed. There can be no doubt about the utility of such arrangements as correct visual accommodation, visual fixation, and optimal adjustment to acoustic stimuli. In those processes internal form pressure elicits the best possible adaptation. Moreover, Gestalt psychology's approach to their explanation is certainly right as opposed to empirical interpretations based on trial and error. But use of the equilibrium concept to explain them is by no means new. It can be traced back to the time when animal behavior was described in terms of tropism.

Löb (1905), the eminent proponent of the theory of tropism, advanced a formulation of how a phototropic insect turns to the light and moves towards it. Assuming that the insect is symmetrically built, it acts in that manner because a state of equilibrium is established in the stimulation of its symmetrically arranged photoreceptors. Whenever the position of the light source changes, the animal's direction changes at the same time, so that the upset balance can be restored to equilibrium. Other tropisms, in addition to phototropism, may be explained in a similar way by reference to equilibrium.

As is well known, the theory of tropism drew considerable adverse criticism half a century ago. The critique was directed against the machine-like compulsion with which animal behavior was said to be governed. It is not at all clear how the Gestalt psychologists would reply to these criticisms. A reply would seem necessary since Gestalt psychology appears to be applying Löb's theory to sensorimotor functions in humans. They do this most obviously in the case of acoustic orientation.

CHAPTER 9

ATTRIBUTES OF FORMS

What are the essential attributes of forms in general? As defined by Gestalt psychology visual figures serve as excellent models. On this basis ten characteristics may be noted:

1. A form is characterized by being separated and standing out in relief. It is closed and structured.

2. A form experience in terms of a figure is an entity which generally cannot be altered arbitrarily by the subject. The more obvious the form, the more it resists alteration by an observer.

3. The whole and its parts mutually determine each other's characteristics. In a phenomenological sense the total form quality dominates the qualities of the parts. The more compact the form is, the more this holds true, not only phenomenologically, but functionally as well.

According to Sander (1926, page 10) a circle is the most compact form. Internal form pressure is revealed with particular clarity when an irregular figure changes in the direction of circularity.

In terms of compactness, to mention an additional example, a straight line follows closely after the ideal circular figure.

4. Minimal simplicity of form is found in the form consisting of a single element. Maximal simplicity is seen when a number of elements are completely articulated in a form.

5. When the parts are less tightly bound together the form quality of the whole tends to disappear.

6. Form perception prevents the observer from separating the parts. On the other hand clear emergence of individual parts disrupts the form impression.

The letters "P" and "D" are not seen in "R" although they enter physically into its construction. Likewise no "F" is seen in "E." The "I" cannot be observed in "R," "P," "E," or "D"; yet it definitely is a part of these letters.

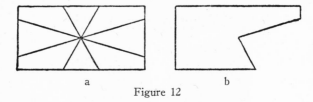

a   b

Figure 12

In optical illusions it is usually impossible to separate out the individual parts which are to be compared. A figure as compact as the Sander parallelogram which was shown in Figure 6b illustrates this fact.

How many observers would see segment **12b** in **12a,** as shown in Figure 12, except by chance?

7. The parts of a form structure have different values. Some are indispensable if wholeness is to be retained. Others are relatively unnecessary.

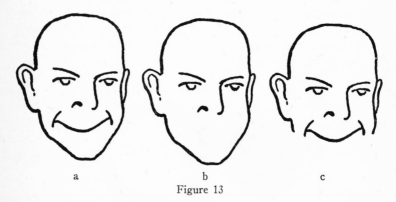

a   b   c

Figure 13

In Figure 13 absence of the mouth completely destroys the characteristic expression of the face. On the other hand leaving out part of the head contour has almost no effect on the expression.

In a caricature the actual relative position and size of features are usually distorted, but individuality of facial expression is not lost in the process. In a dynamic sense every form has its

own focal point; naturally this need not coincide with the geo-
metrical midpoint of the figure.

Figure 14

8. In ambiguous drawings either one of two figures may be
seen. In Figure 14 one sees either a vase or two faces turned
toward each other; both cannot be seen simultaneously. Some
exponents of the older psychology have maintained that in such
instances one figure is noticed while the other figure goes unnoticed for the time being. Gestalt psychology rejects this statement. In general, contours have only a single function, or at any
rate one function at a given time.

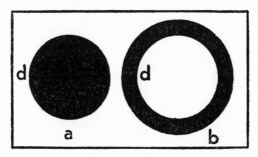

Figure 15

In Figure 15a circle "d" encloses the black disk, but in 15b
circle "d" is in the inner boundary of the round black band.

Marine charts are excellent examples of complete alteration
of ambiguous forms. The alteration depends on the changing

function of a contour. For the same contour in the chart may be
the boundary of either land or water, but never both at the same
time.

The fact that we see *objects* and not the spaces between them,
even if the lines which border on the spaces happen to form
meaningful figures, is bound up with the fact that contours can
perform only one function at a time.

9. Together with the phenomenological primacy of a form
there is a functional primacy as well. Its influence on other
processes stems from the whole, not from its parts. A functional
influence of this sort is shown by the fact that the color threshold
is higher on the figure form than on its background even if the
physical stimulus conditions are identical.

A form strives towards the greatest possible unity and inclusiveness with respect to color and contour. If increased

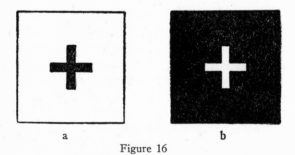

a   b

Figure 16

illumination is projected onto the black cross in Figure 16a, the
threshold will be crossed later than in the case of the equally
black background in 16b when illumination is changed in a
similar manner.

10. In addition to phenomenological and functional primacy
of form there is also genetic primacy, both in an individual and
a general sense. It is individual because form takes precedence
over its elements in the development of each human being. It is
the task of child psychology to demonstrate this. It is general
because form also takes precedence phylogenetically. Social and
comparative psychology testify to that. Thus the form concept
applies to the whole field of genetic psychology.

CHAPTER 10

FIELD THEORY AND MACHINE THEORY

Gestalt psychology rejects the view that sense organs respond to local stimuli with local impressions which are unrelated to other stimuli. Its firm conviction is that the organism reacts as a whole to any given stimulus constellation. The basic assumption is that a form, regarded phenomenologically, is a final and irreducible entity.

The Gestalt theory applied to physiology operates with the field theory developed in physics. At a time when Newton still conceived of forces operating from a distance, Maxwell's field theory considered pull and pressure as forces applied directly from one point to the next. Just as every minor event in an electromagnetic field is related to every other event occurring in it, every minor process in the nervous system is determined by the totality of processes associated with it.

Köhler (1933) states that individual fields have a dynamic interrelationship whose central dynamics play a part in determining the distribution of events as well as their local nature. As far as visual processes are concerned, the entire retina and the nerve segments connected with it are regarded as one unit. Spontaneous self-structuring occurs in a psychophysical field just as it does in a physical field. In the visual sensorium this self-structuring is determined by the physiochemical properties and forces which characterize that modality. However, as seen by Gestalt psychology, the fact that structuring follows dynamic principles and is fully determined does not mean it is a blind, aimless, mechanical process.

It is not only in Gestalt psychology's theory of perception that the field concept plays a leading role. It is also applicable to the whole situation that results from inclusion of the self in the perceptual circumstances. In Köhler's words (1933), "We feel justified in applying the Gestalt concept to the entire area of the self and the tensions between the self and the environment." In this total area the self is usually, but not always, regarded as a notably independent part of a system. The structure of the field may be more or less homogeneous. It must lack homogeneity to at least some extent to permit processes to occur in the first place.

Gestalt psychology has shown great astuteness in refuting the machine theory of the organism. Köhler points out that human beings have always been inclined to assume special mechanical arrangements in nature whenever they came upon order. Aristotle endeavored to explain the orderliness which ruled the heavens. He stated that stars were attached to crystal spheres. When deliberation began about the orderliness which obtains in the human organism it was easy to attribute it to mechanical arrangements. It was supposed that in the nervous system with its precisely established pathways it was the topographical arrangement which prevented disorder.

The older psychology explained definitely circumscribed visual figures by stipulating that the impulses from the retina are conducted to the psychophysical area over isolated, rigidly established paths. Mechanical arrangements were said to guarantee ordered perception. And these mechanical arrangements were supposed to be the basis of order not only in vision, but in every other sense modality as well. They were considered operative from the very first day of life.

When it was discovered that sensory impressions are affected by experiences an individual has in the course of his development, theorists felt compelled to modify the idea of machine-like arrangements. Apparently, it was supposed, they did not prescribe an absolutely definite direction for propagation of impulses, or at least not in earliest childhood. New connecting pathways could develop. But once these new pathways had developed, dynamic factors were ruled out of any further influence on events.

The two views elaborated above maintain that all orderly phenomena in the adult's nervous system depend either on original inherited mechanical structures, namely topological-histological conditions, or on mechanical arrangements developed as the individual grows. On the whole the former version represents the nativistic tendency of the older psychology, while the latter reveals its empirical trend.

Gestalt psychology now believes that its theory of dynamic self-regulation of the psychophysical organism has ended the struggle between the two versions once and for all. As is well known, the battle over them spread to all areas of psychology. For a time it divided psychologists into two hostile camps on the question of spatial psychology. The empiricists maintained that the impression of third dimension is not innate, but develops in the course of experience. The nativists claimed that appreciation of third dimension is inborn and is determined at the very start by innate tendencies. Gestalt psychology rejects this sharp differentiation of the various spatial dimensions, which were carried over from geometry. It is replaced by the more elastic concept that considers rigid separation of the dimensions impossible.

The empiricist assumes that visual fixation develops slowly through experience, while the nativist believes in rigid sensorimotor arrangements for this adjustment. According to Gestalt psychology, the theories of both contestants are based on the view that the sensory apparatus and the motor apparatus are blindly coupled to each other, but with one distinction. For nativism this coupling is on a rigid hereditary basis, whereas for empiricism improved performance depends on experience and practice. Gestalt psychology rejects both assertions, and its standpoint has been expressed in these words: "The sensory system and the motor system are not two separate systems, merely connected by communication pathways. They are parts of one comprehensive system" (Köhler, 1933).

The specific form a process assumes is regulated by the law of pregnance. Gestalt psychology maintains that ocular fixation brings about a better balance among the sensory and motor units of the comprehensive system. The meaningful and purposeful service rendered by optimal presentation of visual stimuli depends on the direction which sensorimotor form phenomena take toward a final state of equilibrium.

Both nativists and empiricists failed to realize that orderly processes in the organism are possible without the assumption of arrangements which are either innate or developed by learning. Vitalism, too, recognized the shortcomings of the machine theory; to explain order it postulated a special vital energy which played a part in physical occurrences. But vitalists, like empiricists and nativists, overlooked the possibility of introducing dynamic self-regulation as an explanatory principle, perhaps because it was borrowed from physics.

Gestalt psychology denies the vitalistic interpretation of order. With its single-minded bent it offers self-structuring of organic processes as its solution of the problem. "Dynamic self-distribution is the sort of functional concept that must be introduced into psychological theory" (Köhler, 1933, page 89). The argument for Gestalt psychology's solution of the problem may best be presented in Köhler's words:

Two varieties of factors constantly determine the course of physical processes. In the first category are forces at work in the process itself; they represent its dynamic aspect. In the second category are those characteristics of the systems concerned which may be regarded as constant conditions for the particular process taking place. In the case of electric current an example of such characteristics would be the spatial arrangement or topography of the conducting materials. In physical systems such conditions can sometimes be dominating, sometimes relatively unimportant. The internal dynamics of the process involved in the electric current example would be decisive in determining its course. On the other hand in machines built by human beings the importance of topographical conditions is almost always so predominant that the role of dynamics is reduced to driving the process along pathways entirely determined by those conditions (1933, page 84).

A machine with its definitely limited freedom contrasts sharply with the natural system of the organism and its capacity for self-regulation without predetermined and rigidly limited scope. Obviously Gestalt psychology does not deny that the organism has certain mechanical arrangements. But they do not extend to the highest level, the psychophysical stratum. For instance, Köhler believes that the ordered arrangement of visual phenomena, as it exists on the retina, persists to the area striata, and that dynamic self-distribution begins beyond that point.

Gestalt psychology commenced its battle against local determination of stimulus effect with reference to an aspect of sense physiology which had already been modified. It was the theory that every point in the sensory field depended exclusively on its local stimulation. That some modification had taken place was made clear by Hering's theory (1905) of the reciprocal action of elements in the visual area. In that formulation the old view of local sensory determination was discarded. A truly rigid mechanical theory could not have been altered in this way.

Hering's dynamic concept applied to color vision. Köhler extended it to all aspects of visual perception, such as perception of form, movement, spatial dimensions, and in fact to all situations in any way connected with the field theory.

The observations made in this chapter serve as a prelude to a discussion of the theory of physical forms and isomorphism.

CHAPTER 11

PHYSICAL FORMS AND ISOMORPHISM

The theory of physical forms, which is among Köhler's (1920) most significant contributions, is one of Gestalt psychology's outstanding concepts. It has stimulated individual research. It has decisively influenced the epistemological and perhaps even the philosophical position of Gestalt psychology.

Leading Gestalt psychologists agree on the main aspects of the new theory, but it is difficult to estimate the extent to which they agree on its details. It is most practical to outline it as presented by its principal exponents.

The theory of physical forms maintains that there are form-like holistic systems in inorganic nature just as there are in biological organisms. This view, if correct, would have important consequences. An apparently insuperable barrier between organic and inorganic processes would be removed. Köhler's interest centered specifically on the separation between psychophysical organic processes and those dealt with in the natural sciences.

It will be recalled that vitalism had introduced a new explanatory principle to overcome the separation of organic and inorganic phenomena. It was an effort to explain those aspects of organic processes which, in the opinion of the vitalists, were not susceptible to interpretation on a physical or chemical basis.

In the course of his investigations of apparent movement as exemplified by the phi phenomenon, Wertheimer (1912) advanced certain hypotheses about the underlying physiological processes involved. He considered them unitary, holistic. His observations did not go beyond introductory speculation based on the "short circuit" concept. It was then that Köhler postulated the theory of isomorphism.

The essence of isomorphism is that phenomenologically ascertained forms actually correspond to psychophysical forms. Psychophysical forms in the brain are viewed as not essentially different from the physical forms of inorganic nature. The significance of the formulation is clear. Physical forms are obviously approachable by physical methods of investigation. And if the forms of experience correspond to recognizable physical forms in the nervous system, a path is opened to the study of the brain processes concerned. It is an approach which promises far more reliable results than the more or less speculative methods of the older psychology.

To prove the existence of forms in the inorganic world Köhler applied both of Ehrenfels' (1890) criteria for experienced forms. He maintained that they could be employed equally well in the case of physical forms. Briefly, physical forms were said to be more than "*and*-connections," and transposable. An example offered to show that the two criteria can be met is the distribution of a given quantity of electricity in an isolated conductor of definite shape.

In the first place the distribution of electricity under the conditions mentioned is not a mere "*and*-connection." Rather it is a physical system in which every part is related to every other part. At no place in the conductor can a quantity of electricity be removed or added without causing a redistribution of the electricity in the entire system. Its physical pattern reacts as a whole and thus satisfies the first criterion contributed by Ehrenfels.

In the second place the transposability of the electric system is shown by the fact that its characteristic structure is retained even if the quantity of electricity is changed and redistribution results. Moreover, the fact of transposability is shown in still another way. The characteristic structure of the charge is not altered even if the carrier, whether it be a wire, plate, or other form, is enlarged or made smaller without changing its geometric pattern.

Electrostatic forms are of special interest because brain processes are demonstrably electric in nature. This accounts for Köhler's choice of electric phenomena as illustrations.

Köhler's arguments against the machine theory are supported by investigations of physical forms. They show "that order in extensive physical forms does not require binding together of local processes which pursue unalterable, predestined, isolated paths. Order is possible and actually occurs by means of spontaneous self-structuring of related physical systems" (1933).

Turning now to the theory of isomorphism, it is appropriate to begin with a reference to Johannes Müller (1837), the founder of modern physiology. He offered the hypothesis that the essence of the somatic processes underlying perception was manifested in the perceptual circumstances themselves. There was said to be an understandable relationship between the two.

Starting with Johannes Müller's view, G. E. Müller (1896) and Hering (1905) gave further consideration to the nature of the brain processes which might account for color vision. Hering took the position that white, red, and yellow were associated with catabolism, while the three complementary colors, black, green, and blue, were related to anabolism.

Gestalt psychology paid little attention to the sense data itself, and concentrated instead on its form. The same interest in structure is apparent in Gestalt psychology's theory of isomorphism, which deals with the correspondence between phenomena as experienced and their physiological correlates. "Our working hypothesis states that the specific arrangement of actual experience is an accurate reproduction of a dynamically functioning arrangement of the corresponding physiological brain processes" (Köhler, 1933). The structural characteristics of consciousness are in every instance related to corresponding psychophysical processes. The two are connected in a meaningful way. Köhler's theory of isomorphism goes so far as to conjecture that "it will be shown that the phenomenal world is literally the expression of circumstances in the brain" (1933).

It was in conjunction with isomorphism that Köhler touched on the unity of the senses, a theory which has attracted steadily increasing interest. The theory maintains that various sense modalities are not separated by a gap that cannot be bridged, as was believed by Helmholtz and others. On the contrary, they are said to be connected by certain attributes common to them all. Brightness and dullness of impressions are examples of such attributes. Köhler attempted to account for the relationship of sense fields by suggesting that relevant chemical changes in the central physiological processes are approximately similar.

Two noteworthy aspects of isomorphism remain to be discussed. The first is the subordination of the parts of a physical form to the whole they help constitute. This subordination would be the counterpart of similar subjection of the parts of a psychological form, as previously described. Köhler describes the relationship of parts to the whole in physical forms by citing another example in the field of electrostatics: "If a square metal plate holds an electric charge its density varies considerably in various parts of the plate. It is greater at the edges than in the center, and greatest of all at the corners. If the metal plate is placed in a comparatively large spherical flask, the charge will be equalized over the entire area" (1933). Thus the same part, in this case the charged plate, varies in various whole situations. In another example the charged square plate becomes a "weak," loosely constructed form if it is connected with a charged sphere by means of a long, thin wire. Then the sphere participates in the system, but determines only the amount of the total charge to be held by the plate. The plate, nevertheless, retains its own characteristic density distribution.

The second aspect of physical forms to be described is their tendency toward precision and maximal simplicity. Again the effort is to note that physical forms duplicate certain striking qualities of psychological forms. Köhler points out that "if a current passes through a wire lying on a flat, isolated surface it assumes a circular form regardless of its previous shape. The conductor, the flow of current, and the field arrange themselves in space with maximal symmetry and simplicity" (1933).

Another physical phenomenon which demonstrates the tendency of an unstable form toward one which is better balanced is presented by Köhler: "If one pours oil into a liquid of equal density, but a kind with which the oil will not mix, surface tensions alter the shape of the boundary lines until the oil floats in the other liquid in the form of a sphere. This occurs because of dynamic processes at the boundary of the two liquids" (1933, page 88). In this striving to become more regular and to abandon asymmetry, Köhler sees the objective basis for the fact that the tendency toward regularity and symmetry is also revealed in experienced, psychological forms.

Quite clearly the form concept extends far beyond the field of psychology. It reaches into physics and physiology as well.

CHAPTER 12

DYNAMIC INTERPRETATION OF SPACE

One contribution to a dynamic theory of acoustic spatial localization has already been indicated. It is the fact that the ears can react to minute differences in stimulation time. Acting in two capacities, they respond to these differences in time with an impression of direction.

The problem of acoustic localization is notably different from the question of a dynamic approach to visual space. Gestalt psychology has substituted this dynamic viewpoint for the geometric concept which was at one time more common.

It might be said, on the one hand, that sound experiences conjure up acoustic space "out of nothing." On the other hand the space-creating powers of binocular vision operate on original space already at hand, and transform it. An example of such transformation of an original spatial experience is the subjective visual gray. It appears when the visual receptors are removed from all environmental influences. It represents an internal equilibrium arrived at when the lids are closed and protected from light. Proper introspection will convince anyone that the subjective visual gray seems to be on a wall-like surface some distance directly ahead. The surface is slightly concave and is bounded, although it is difficult to fix the boundaries precisely. Even this original visual space goes through characteristic changes under the influence of internal forces. Such changes take place, for instance, if the subject voluntarily converges his eyes more by imagining a nearer fixation point. As a result the visual field becomes distinctly narrower and moves closer. At the same time the gray becomes darker and its surface more dense. These phenomena reveal the existence of an internal dynamics of visual space. The operation of external factors is shown when the eyes are open and consequent retinal images are examined. Under those circumstances visual space as originally given is altered to a marked degree by convergence, crossed disparation, accommodation, and other processes.

Motion makes possible the comprehension of aspects of spatial perception which would remain completely hidden under ordinary circumstances. Yet this factor has been neglected up to this time. It will be recalled that Chapter 6, entitled "Gestalt Laws," described experiments which made use of two projectors. In the last-mentioned of these investigations the movement of the two groups of projected dots was seen simultaneously, in the same location, as one impression of movement on the same plane. The impression was not of two movements either on the same plane or one behind the other. The latter situation occurs very seldom under usual visual conditions, and certainly never in a pure form. The artificial, or at least unusual, nature of those circumstances can be made clear by considering a specific example: A fish is seen moving in clear water; simultaneously, and in the same visual space, a different movement—naturally an inverted image—is seen reflected from the smooth surface of the water. This illustration is helpful, but can by no means be considered an everyday matter, and can hardly lead to a reliable conclusion about the nature of simultaneous perception of two movements in the same place.

A technically satisfactory solution of the problem mentioned can be reached with the aid of three projectors, one or two of which may be for motion pictures. This equipment affords convincing proof that under appropriate conditions two or even three movements can be perceived in the same location, or one behind the other. There follows a report on the rewarding but complex procedures employed by Rehnberg under the writer's direction:

Three projectors are set up in such a way that one is aimed directly at the screen and the other two face it from a slightly different angle. The projectors have been rebuilt to allow endless strips of perfectly transparent plastic to be passed through the slide chambers at variable speeds. Each of the three plastic strips has a different pattern, which is repeated along its sur-

face; the repeated patterns consist of black outlines whose surfaces are colored. Three samples of these patterns may be seen
in Figure 17. The three directions of the shading in the figure
symbolize the fact that three different colors—red, blue, and
yellow—are used.

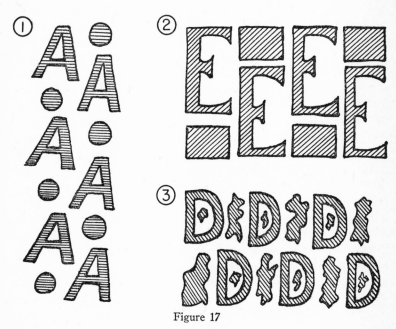

Figure 17

In the experimental procedure all three patterns glide across
the same area of the screen at the same time. The first moves
from left to right, the second from the top toward the bottom,
and the third travels in a diagonal direction. In the course of
this action the subject sees three distinct movements taking
place simultaneously. One is seen distinctly while the other two
are less clear. The movements permeate each other in a singular
manner which is difficult to describe; they seem to take place on
the same plane or in the same direction. Proof that the eyes are
capable of such performance sheds new light on the plasticity of
the organism, in this instance in the field of visual perception.

Another opportunity to study two movements which occur

in the same place or behind each other is afforded by the frequently employed motion picture technique of having two scenes overlap. As one fades out the other becomes more vivid until it has completely replaced the first. The writer applied this method with encouraging results.

Motion pictures were taken of individuals walking past a uniform background. A new film was then prepared by copying one strip of an individual walking in one direction; a mirror image of the same original scene was then superimposed on this copy. Projection of the resulting film showed the same person simultaneously walking from left to right and from right to left, apparently passing through himself in the center of the picture as if he were made of air, and then separating again. Plate 1 is a sample segment of the film and shows the effect achieved. This photographic procedure gives a definite impression of two movements occurring on the same plane, and is truly striking. It is conceivable that this phenomenon, which might be termed a "mirror image effect," could be used for surrealistic motion picture techniques.

At this juncture it appears appropriate to note certain facts indicating that spatial perception is influenced by pregnance tendencies which have received almost no recognition. Spatial experience is always determined by the relationship of environmental objects to each other as well as their position with respect to the observer. Many easily accomplished observations clearly reveal that both aspects of spatial perception respond to internal pressure; the result is that the experience centers on a point where a line extending straight ahead from the eyes crosses a line perpendicular to it, a frontal-parallel line.

The report which follows is restricted to findings which demonstrate the pregnance tendency as it affects localization of perceptual objects by the observer.

For purposes of investigation photographs were made of model houses, trees, persons, and animals. They were of the type found in playrooms of child guidance clinics, where children use them to construct more or less complex "worlds." Plates 2, 3, and 4 show the same scene viewed from different angles. Photographs of this sort provide an excellent means of studying

Plate 1

Plate 2

Plate 3

Plate 4

the laws of perspective, as well as the development of children's spatial concepts.

In an experiment conducted by two of the writer's students, Schildt and Pettersson, children were required to reproduce the scenes with materials provided for that purpose. The greatest success, and at the earliest age level, was achieved in the case of Plate 2. Only the older children were able to reproduce in concrete form the obliquity of the remaining two scenes. Younger children are not equal to these tasks. As a rule they respond by copying Plates 3 and 4 as if they were straight ahead, on a plane parallel to the two eyes. This departure from an oblique image of environmental structure, and toward a frontal-parallel view, is an expression of pregnance. With Plate 4 as a model there is also a tendency—found less often, it is true—to build in the direction of the median plane. This is significant since the deviation of the picture's axis from the frontal-parallel plane is considerably greater than its deviation from the median plane. It may be concluded that the spatial concepts of children clearly tend toward the frontal-parallel and median planes as preferred directions.

Obviously the procedures which made use of the photographs are not suitable for demonstrating adults' internal pressure toward the two preferred planes of visual space. In the case of adult subjects other methods are more appropriate, and are patterned after the procedures previously described, in which the surroundings of a color area were varied. In those experiments the color area was detached from all possible color forms. The simple method to be outlined requires that a three-dimensional model be detached from all rigid spatial relationships.

A horizontal surface was revolved by a motor with variable speed. "Worlds" consisting of more or less complex materials, such as cubes, cylinders, etc., were placed on the revolving surface. The adult subject observed this display and was required to use appropriate materials to reproduce the "world" he saw on the turning platform by building it on a table. It should be emphasized that the subject never saw the model at rest. It was already revolving at full speed when he first observed it, and continued in motion throughout the period of building activity.

Thus no position of the model was distinguished from any other as far as the observer was concerned; perceptually all the positions of the revolving scene were equal. By means of this procedure a portion of the external world was detached from its relationships to its surroundings, and at the same time removed from a fixed orientation to the observer. The subject naturally was forced to decide upon a specific position for his copy of the turning scene. The decision is a noteworthy one.

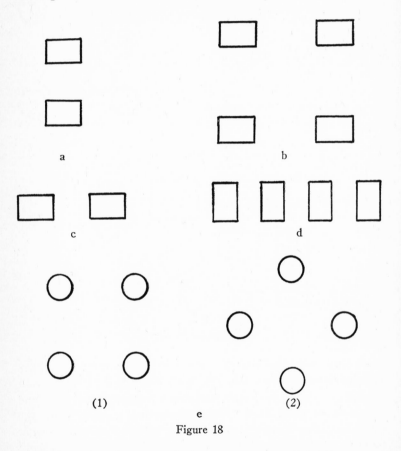

Figure 18

In the case of symmetrical arrangements of the structural elements the subjects chose, with almost no exception, a frontal-parallel position or one perpendicular to it. Patterns of houses, for instance, were reproduced as shown diagrammatically in Figure 18a, b, c, and d. When four upright wooden cylinders were used, as shown in Figure 18e, Position 1 was chosen far more often, with Position 2 in second place. No other varia-

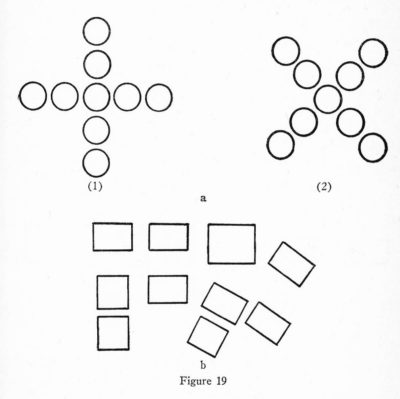

(1)   (2)

a

b

Figure 19

tions occurred. The use of nine cylinders revealed a definite preference for Position 1 in 19a, with Position 2 of 19b next in frequency. Again no other variations appeared. If the scene was asymmetrical, as in 19b, representing a street plan, the rotation method produced enlightening insight into spatial structuring. It was determined in part by internal "geographical" relationships of the grouping, and in part by the individual nature of the subject.

The detailed dynamics of visual space is amply treated in Gestalt literature. It will be more profitable to clarify the dynamic approach to tactile and kinesthetic spatial impressions. Those related to the body image have been particularly neglected.

The term "body image" refers to the spatial image of the self, which each individual constructs on the basis of all the sensations originating in various parts of the body at rest and in motion. The image consists of the parts of the body and their spatial relationships to each other.

A number of investigations of the so-called phantom limb have helped to explain how the body image develops (Katz, 1921). The case of an individual who has lost the greater part of one arm will be considered as an example. He may still experience the most realistic sensations in the missing limb. The illusion sometimes persists for many years.

All parts of the phantom limb are not sensed with equal acuity. The hand makes the most vivid impressions. The illusory perceptions become weaker and weaker towards the stump. Moreover, sensations ascribed to joints are experienced more clearly than those which seem to originate in the limb segments between the joints.

Facts observed in the case of a phantom arm also hold true for the phantom leg. Again the distal part, the foot, is sensed most distinctly. In some instances the amputee retains only the phantom hand or foot. It is experienced as if it were suspended in space at some distance from the stump and not connected with it.

The phantom limb gives rise to curious conjectures since its spatial arrangement and other characteristics are unique. If an amputee walks up to a wall the phantom limb seems to go through it. He "feels" the phantom limb where he actually sees the wall, and the law of the impermeability of matter does not seem to hold.

It has been assumed that the phantom experience arises from stimuli in the nerve endings of the stump. However, a more precise explanation would certainly involve physiological residues in the central nervous system. These determine the qualitative aspects of the phantom as well as its spatial characteristics. The strength of the residues can be deduced from the vividness of various parts of phantom limbs. Such differences lead to the conclusion that the residues for the distal parts are stronger than those for proximal parts, and that joint residues are stronger than those representing intermediate segments.

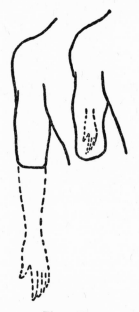

Figure 20

With the passage of time characteristic changes occur in a phantom limb. It must be assumed that they are caused by the dynamics of the residual field. The phantom tends to shrink. It becomes smaller and smaller and sometimes a hand approaches the size of a child's. As it shrinks the phantom limb draws closer to the stump. Eventually it moves completely into the stump, as is suggested by Figure 20.

What causes a phantom limb to shrink? The change does not depend on nerve tissues of the stump, but on the residual fields of the brain. Apparently forces are at work which begin to operate only when loss of the limb causes loss of those peripheral influences which insure normal experience for the body part concerned. A rubber balloon supplies an analogy for the process. It retains its tension as long as gas pressure is maintained. It begins to shrink as soon as this pressure decreases. The elastic balloon represents the surface of the limb, while the "tensions"—represented by the gas pressure—are caused by all the tactile, kinesthetic, and other impressions which the limb mediates in the course of normal activity. If this external "tension" is abolished, the tendencies of the residual field gain the upper hand and allow the limb to shrink until an equilibrium is reached.

There is much to be said for the view that the phantom limb's regression throws light on the original structuring of arm and leg impressions in the life of each individual. It does this by reversing the growth process. Wilhelm Stern (1935) designates the neonate's oral zone, which establishes the first critical contact with the environment, as the infant's original tactile-kinesthetic space impression. Starting with that, the body image grows as a result of passive and active movements which occur in the body and its extensions. Development of the child's body image progresses more rapidly when he begins to use his hands more purposefully. It is quite conceivable that a child senses his hands as comparatively isolated from the oral zone and not connected with the body, just as the phantom hands of some amputees seem isolated from the stumps.

The importance of hands in the individual's development explains their greater vividness in phantom limbs. After beginning to use his hands, the next most important advance in the child's conquest of space occurs when he starts to walk. The feet, in turn, are the next most significant parts of the body image because they afford contact with the ground. And again this significance is reflected in the impressive nature of the foot in a phantom limb experience.

The phantom limb may well make a major contribution to an understanding of how the body image develops.

CHAPTER 13

PROPRIOCEPTIVE REFLEX AND VOLUNTARY ACTION

Scientists with varied viewpoints have given their attention to the relationship between proprioceptive reflexes and voluntary action. Gestalt psychology, too, has attempted to clarify this problem. Two illustrations will provide a basis for discussion:

If the reader holds his hand open with his fingers spread out, and then quickly moves the fingers together, he will observe that they involuntarily spring apart again. A similar reaction occurs if the forearm is first bent and then quickly extended. The result is an immediate, involuntary recoil of the forearm. Such limb movements are instances of what Sherrington (1947) termed "proprioceptive reflex actions." Innervation of a contracted muscle is associated with central inhibition of the antagonistic muscle concerned. But this inhibition is immediately followed by central excitation which evokes contraction of the temporarily relaxed antagonistic muscle. Sherrington designated this type of response as "secondary induction." The process was known before Sherrington studied it. Physiologists knew it as an "antagonistic reflex," but were unable to explain it in a satisfactory way.

Proprioceptive reflex movements play an important part in the so-called tapping test, in which the subject taps as rapidly as he can with one finger. It can easily be demonstrated that this act does not require intent to perform each separate finger movement. On the contrary, the actual conscious intent is the instruction, "Tap as rapidly as possible." This sets the finger in motion and keeps it active as long as is desired. The determination sets in motion a self-regulating mechanism which requires no attention to each of its component movements. The tapping movements can be described as voluntary, but not in the sense that every single movement is subject to will and guided by it. Movement should be termed voluntary only if its smallest component is executed in accordance with a specific intention applied to it. In reality a movement whose separate parts are individually controlled can never be carried out quickly (Katz and Künnapas, 1946).

It can be stated without exaggeration that almost every limb movement executed with great speed is associated with an antagonistic reflex. Its importance in voluntary movement has been admirably formulated by Isserlin: "Intent in voluntary movement continually allows for antagonistic reaction by putting it to use, avoiding it, curtailing it, or allowing it to run its course unhindered" (1910).

Antagonistic reaction is equally significant in movements which have become automatic and whose speed is over a certain minimum. A searching investigation led Wachholder (1925) to believe that individual movements cannot be regarded as the most elementary units, and that more complex movements are not built by combinations of them. He states that "paired reciprocal movements should be considered the elementary form of physiological motor action. Individual movements, whether voluntary or reflex, should be regarded as complex secondary modifications of original rhythmic functioning. Viewed in this manner, execution of the simplest individual movement is by no means the most elementary motor task, but a highly complicated act in which intent imposes an entirely foreign mode of reaction on the physiological motor mechanism."

Observation of young infants readily reveals that all the rapid movements they carry out with their limbs actually are reciprocal movements. Whenever they make voluntary arm or leg movements, proprioceptive reflexes make their appearance. This fact is of great significance for Gestalt psychology. It means that the most primitive motor unit is not a single movement in one direction, which might be regarded as the motor "atom." Rather it is a paired reciprocal movement. It is noteworthy that a child finds it very difficult to learn to suppress reciprocal movement and adopt controlled movement in its place.

CHAPTER 14

PERCEPTION OF THE BODILY SELF

Sensations from the muscles, tendons, joints, semicircular canals, and the eyes all play a part in structuring our subjective bodily impressions. If these sensations are not referred to the bodily self, but are objectified instead, they produce information about the environment. They indicate whether objects are rough or smooth, elastic or rigid, light or heavy. However, it should be noted that subjective referral of sensations involves Gestalt laws which are entirely different from those which operate when the same sensations are projected outward. This fact can be demonstrated by a comparison of outwardly directed activities and those in the course of which one part of the body acts on another part.

Clenching the teeth or holding an object in one hand, or with both hands, are examples of one body segment stimulating another. In pincers-like activities such as those, the subject underestimates the pressure he applies. The underestimation may be enormous and presents a sharp contrast to situations which require energy to be directed outward. A pressure of 44 pounds exerted on a dynamometer may be judged equal to the pull of a freely movable object weighing 6⅔ pounds. In a similar way the subject underestimates the pressure of his bite when his jaws press against each other, as well as the force exerted by his hands as they grasp an object (Katz, 1943).

As a rule pincers-like activity is associated with pressure directed outward. Most work done while standing alters the pressure and push relationship between the soles of the feet and the floor. This change is illustrated by the marked shift of forces which occurs in the soles when an ax is used.

The close ties between manual activity and activity of the feet has been almost entirely overlooked. As is the case with the most varied sorts of bodily movements, manual acts always have an effect on the contact surface of the foot and the floor.

Experiments have shown that even great variations of pincers-like activities have little effect on the evaluation of pressure directed outward. Four procedures will be described:

1. The subject is required to lift weights by means of grips which register variations in pressure exerted on them. Judgment of the weights is only slightly affected by an objective shift in their value ranging from $1\frac{1}{5}$ to $4\frac{2}{5}$ pounds. Judgment of the amount of pressure exerted on the grips varies little although the actual pressure change may be as great as from $4\frac{2}{5}$ to $24\frac{4}{5}$ pounds. Even when two acts—lifting and pressing—are as closely linked as they are in this experiment, the subject's evaluation of the force he exerts in each remains separate and follows different principles. Expressed in Gestalt terms, there is little communication between the two action systems.

2. Two scales are placed side by side. The subject stands with one foot on each scale, but distributes his weight so that one leg supports most of it. The other leg bears such a small part of the weight that it may be termed a "mock leg." Under these circumstances the "mock leg" may carry as much as $\frac{1}{5}$ of the total body weight when the subject reports that it bears almost none. An individual who weighs 165 pounds may think his "mock leg" carries none of his weight at all, although the scale indicates that the sole of his foot exerts a pressure of as much as 33 pounds. He senses contact with the sole but has no distinct pressure experience.

3. The subject stands barefoot on a scale and grasps a horizontal bar with both hands. He either pulls or pushes so that pressure on the scale is alternately decreased and increased to a marked degree. Nevertheless the subject observes astonishingly little change in pressure on his soles as a result of the pulling and pushing described. If he weighs 165 pounds and pressure on the scale decreases to about 55 pounds followed by an increase to about 275 pounds, the variation is as 1 is to 5. Yet the experienced change is insignificant.

4. The subject stands barefoot on a scale and alternately bends his knees and stands erect. These movements cause con-

siderable variation in pressure on the scale. The size of the variations depends on the speed and energy with which the movements are carried out. If the subject bends his knees very suddenly pressure on his soles may decline to zero. On the other hand if an individual who weighs 165 pounds rises quickly the pressure may be as much as 330 pounds. It is surprising to discover that even with such extreme variation, again as 1 is to 5, the subject perceives almost no change whatsoever.

The experiments described seem to indicate that the soles are remarkably insensitive to absolute as well as relative differences in pressure. Yet the soles are particularly well supplied with pressure receptors.

Interestingly enough an entirely different result is obtained if pressure sensitivity of the soles is measured while the subject lies on his back. The smaller the surface that is pressed against his bare foot, the lower the absolute pressure threshold for change becomes. If the surface is about one square centimeter a pressure of .55 pound produces a distinct pressure experience. But if pressure is applied to the entire sole a distinct pressure experience results only when the objective pressure amounts to 2.2 pounds. This figure—2.2 pounds—is noteworthy when it is recalled that the subject in Experiment 2, resting part of his weight on a "mock leg," did not report a pressure experience when the objective pressure actually was 15 times 2.2!

For a reclining subject the pressure threshold is approximately 25 per cent. However, according to Experiments 2 and 3, in which the circumstances are different, the threshold is seen to be 500 per cent or even more. Is there an unresolvable contradiction in these findings? There is a contradiction only if one starts with acceptance of the constancy hypothesis. The assumption would then be that the same sensory stimulus must always evoke the same sensory experience, without regard for other occurrences in the sensory field. But the constancy hypothesis has been shown to be unacceptable. There never are isolated stimuli. There are only those stimuli which, together with more stimuli of the same—or other—sense modalities, form organized total patterns. Hence there are no pressure stimuli on the soles, as such. There are only pressure stimuli set in a complex stimulus field. And the field itself varies with vertical and horizontal posture, relative rest and exercise, with the position of the feet and departures from a particular position. Total bodily experience changes in each of these circumstances. Furthermore, this total bodily experience is obviously the most inclusive form connected with the bodily self. It is only with reference to that all-embracing form that its constituent, segmental forms receive their values.

Under precisely what circumstances does stimulation of sense organs contribute to a unitary body experience? They make such a contribution in so far as they are subjectified. Accepting the distinction between subjective and objective referral of impressions, it can be said that the pressure sensations evoked from the soles in the scale experiments are in the subjective sphere. They are objectified only in the last experiment in which the subject reclined. As long as contact between soles and floor is maintained in a standing position, the resulting stimuli become part of the bodily experience. However, in a reclining position pressure is sensed as coming from without and is objectified. It remains on the periphery of the individual's bodily perceptions. In a sense it is as if an object touched one's forehead or hand.

It would appear that of all stimuli applied to the soles, the only ones subject to the Gestalt principles are those which determine total bodily experience. Sensations of pressure on the soles apparently lack any great power of penetration. That is why the marked variations described go unnoticed. Their difference threshold, in contrast to the difference threshold for objectified pressure, is extremely high.

CHAPTER 15

DYNAMIC SELF-REGULATION IN FOOD SELECTION

Hunger is more transparent and more accessible to investigation than other cyclical psychophysical processes, such as the sex drive, because the connections between experienced hunger and the corresponding physiological phenomena are fairly well known. One important aspect of the hunger drive is the problem of food selection.

The writer has had occasion to employ the principle of dynamic self-regulation of the organism to clarify instinctive food selection. It should be pointed out that food selection may be termed instinctive when it is effected without insight into its purpose and cannot be explained by trial and error in individual experience.

There are striking instances of food selection which have the special characteristics of instinctive behavior, but are not in accord with either of the prevailing empirical or nativistic instinct theories. Among these are perversions of appetite. Illustrations are bone eating, known as osteophagy, among cattle, wool eating by sheep, devouring of their own young by rats in confinement or by foxes on fur ranches.

A particularly noteworthy example of instinctive food selection is seen in the way certain animals "take medicine" when they are ill or poisoned. They consume vegetable matter which contains an effective remedy, but which they apparently do not eat when they feel well.

In both cases the organism provides itself with the substances it lacks either because they happen not to be in the usual food or because of an exceptional need for them.

Individual experience in the empirical sense fails to explain either case because the animal solves the problem facing it at once. This promptness is reminiscent of the speed with which an amputated animal alters its motor behavior in an adaptive manner. On the other hand it can hardly be assumed, in the nativistic sense, that specific chemical tendencies, inherited from previous generations, are revealed in the purposeful behavior of the animals. It is the principle of dynamic self-regulation which points the way out of the difficulty. Just as the function of the spinal cord changes from one moment to the next, the organism's chemical state is subject to continual variation. It changes in such a way that the animal becomes sensitized to substances which were previously neutral. They acquire positive valence and are ingested.

The destiny of animals is determined by a chemical dynamism which—as is seen in the structuring of perception—is amazingly adaptable and does justice to a large number of unusual situations. Naturally the situations are not unlimited in scope. Animals may, and at times do, eat lethal poisons for which "no grass is grown." The "wisdom of the body" is confounded by every fatality of that nature.

The dynamic concept elaborated above is not empirical. Yet it grants the influence of experience just as much free play as the Gestalt psychology of perception concedes in the structuring of objects.

The observations offered may be extended to form a more general theory of instinctive food selection. It cannot be based on the assumption that an animal has inherited tendencies to take the same food that was taken by earlier generations. Rather, it can be suggested that in a situation which is usual for a species it makes food selections which the zoologist reports as typical. This selection can operate in a freakish manner, as evidenced by the koala bear of New Zealand, which eats only eucalyptus leaves. But it is in accord with the principle of dynamic self-regulation in a chemical sense. It is the selection best suited to maintenance of the organism's chemical equilibrium, since it fills a need.

Störring (1931) cites a classical example of chemo-dynamic self-regulation, although he does not call attention to its significance for that specific problem. A young mechanic, B, became a victim of gas poisoning, and from that time on was unable to recall any impressions for more than about two seconds. He had completely lost the ability to learn from experience and make normal use of it. A few of Störring's many interesting findings will be reported here to show how B's attitude towards food was determined by organic states under conditions in which conscious memory played no part.

B's attitude towards eating remained normal. He came to meals at the proper time because hunger and thirst compelled him to do so. When satisfaction of the body's most vital needs is concerned the individual's memory is by no means as important as was thought by the associationists. The organism fills its needs of its own accord by means of self-regulation based on chemical, psychological, and physiological factors.

B never overate. He stopped eating when he had taken a reasonable amount of food. At that point the food before him no longer had positive valence. In fact B was more sensible than many normal persons, who frequently eat or drink too much.

With instinctive certainty B knew what to eat and drink, as is shown clearly in the case of his fondness for beer. When his organism told him he had drunk enough, he stopped. Once, when he had beer with his luncheon and it was again offered to him at the next meal, he declined and said he would prefer water. He behaved as if he knew he had enough beer at noon. He most certainly was not conscious of the situation, but his organism "knew" it.

While recuperating from a surgical operation B acted wisely. He stayed in bed as long as seemed objectively desirable, and of his own accord. He kept a diet that was appropriate in view of the operation. He did this without realizing that he had undergone an operation, that his diet was in any way different, and without knowing why he was in bed in the first place. A clearer example of what chemical self-regulation of the organism can do could hardly be desired.

CHAPTER 16

TRANSFORMATION OF THE GESTALT

Gestalt psychology indicates that visual forms usually are perceived involuntarily. The stronger the form, the greater the compulsion to perceive it in a specific manner, and the greater the effort required to transform it.

A comparison of the three sections in Figure 21 shows that

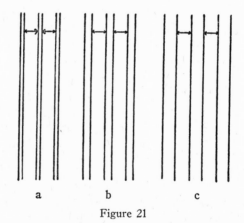

Figure 21

the pairs of lines in "a" stand out more clearly than those in "b," and that these in turn are more obvious than the pairs in "c." However, it is possible to resist that particular form impression and see the lines differently. It can be accomplished by pairing the lines indicated by double arrows. Clearly enough it is more easily done in the case of "c" than "a." The new formation then displaces the original one which arose spontaneously, but only when the observer actively intervenes in the process.

What is the significance of activity which leads to reorganization of forms? The activity itself is just as real as the new form it brings into being. Gestalt psychology explains form reorganization in this manner:

"From a functional point of view such a change of attitude may be due to a physiological vector from other parts of the brain area; it is directed towards its receptors and within certain limits is able to reorganize the field."

The writer cannot regard this formulation as a completely satisfactory effort to explain mental activity which plays a part in transforming a figure. It simply substitutes a "process" for an "activity." Phenomenologically considered, a process is by no means equivalent to the experience of activity.

Spontaneity and activity are not confined to such minor instances as visual figures; they play a part in every spontaneous thought process and in the experiences designated as voluntary acts. But Gestalt psychology is helpless in dealing with such phenomena. Naturally it rejects the reflex approach. But many formulations which are a consequence of field theory suggest that Gestalt psychology interprets mental processes in a quasi-reactive manner, as if they were largely nondeliberate.

The assumption of mental activity and its accompanying multiple stratification of the mind could hardly be agreeable to Gestalt psychology with its single-minded outlook. Yet it is impossible to deny just that sort of multiple stratification. It can reveal itself in various ways. For instance, a fully conscious individual not only has experiences, but is clearly aware of having them. He knows that he "intends." He can stand off from his experiences and make them objects of his reflection. In this way the subject can see forms not only in the sense that the forms "have him," but he can also be quite certain that it is he who "has the forms." As Stern stated, "There is no form apart from the subject who forms it."

Can it be that Gestalt psychology has shunned the problem of multiple stratification of consciousness because it is difficult for isomorphism to solve it? Precisely what would correspond to intention, as seen by an isomorphism that recognizes only "process" and no "activity"? Scheerer is entirely correct when he states that "intending" cannot be reduced to "occurring." As matters stand there is no conceivable physiological happening which could be the true basis of intent.

Children behave in a far more reactive manner than do adults. In younger children there is no such thing as reflection on experience, a fact which raises the question of how reflection and intention develop. For the present there can be no positive answer. In any event the fact that reflection and intention do not occur in younger children makes child psychology more accessible to a Gestalt approach. For the same reason there are good prospects for applying Gestalt views to the behavior of primitive peoples.

Even more than child psychology and the psychology of primitive peoples, comparative psychology should prove the ideal field for application of Gestalt theory. An animal never leaves the magic circle in which it is imprisoned by its perceptions, drives, and instincts. The more naturally a psychological process runs its course, the better it is adapted to interpretation in the light of Gestalt psychology. On the other hand, the more a human being departs from the natural state, whether through maturation or participation in cultural values, the less Gestalt psychology alone, working with the concept of isomorphism, can do justice to him.

The outcome of a Gestalt approach to child psychology, comparative psychology, and the psychology of primitive peoples will be the subject matter of later chapters.

CHAPTER 17

UNDERSTANDING SUBJECTIVE RESPONSES OF OTHER PERSONS

The older psychology assumed that an individual ascribes emotions, ideas, and other experiences to fellow humans on the basis of analogy with those he perceives in himself. This remarkable view still finds some acceptance. The outlook of Gestalt psychology on this question is close to that of Klages (1935), Scheler (1926), and Plessner (1923). They agree in rejecting the older psychology's view.

The association psychologists maintained that we observe certain bodily movements in ourselves at times when we experience mental states such as joy, sorrow, and disappointment. When we then see another individual displaying similar bodily movements we conclude that he, too, knows joy, sorrow, and disappointment. The theory is another example of the extreme empiricism which characterized the older psychology. It assumes only a superficial bond between the subjective state and its corresponding expressive movements. On that basis only repeated analogical judgments, continually confirmed in experience, could lead to understanding of others. This older view is untenable. It can be refuted by principles of general psychology and by contemplating the unsatisfactory results to which it leads in child psychology and animal psychology.

What can be said for the claim that the subject can establish an empirical bond between his experiences and the expressive movements of his own body? It is true that he sees a great many of his arm and leg movements. But he perceives changes of his facial expression only on those comparatively rare occasions when a mirror is available. How many persons have even once looked into a mirror to watch themselves cry? An actor feigning tears might do this, but who else? When would a child have an opportunity to study his expressive movements in a mirror? These questions would be sufficient refutation. However, there is the added absurdity of assuming that animals, too, have an opportunity to perceive their own expressive movements, reflect on them, and are able to understand their fellow creatures on this basis.

It happens that children actually do possess an excellent understanding of friendliness, disapproval, and other attitudes which find expression in the features of those around them. Kaila (1935) indicates that even very young children demonstrate comprehension of that sort. Comparative psychology has ample evidence of mutual comprehension of the expressive movements which regulate behavior between mates, parents and young, friend and foe. These findings cannot possibly be brought into accord with the hypothesis of judgment by analogy. Comprehension of the experiences of others must be largely primitive even if it is at times modified and refined by experience.

Verbal expression is of prime importance in the modification and refinement of social understanding. But all expressive movements which are common to human beings in every culture and do not depend on verbal expression may be considered innate and innately comprehensible. It is expression that a creature in an early stage of development grasps first of all in the welter of environmental events. Physiognomical, not cognitive, attributes of the environment are primary. The principle applies just as much to comprehension of inanimate objects as it does to understanding living organisms. As Wertheimer states: "An object is just as sinister as it is black; in fact it is sinister first of all."

Another fallacy of the analogous conclusion hypothesis is the assumption that an individual pictures to himself the subjective experience of others at every possible opportunity. Certainly that is not true of everyday life. Comprehension on the basis of facial expression and behavior is far more superficial. The visible expression of the other person is understood, and is quite sufficient. We displace his expression inward and locate it within him, but not necessarily in his consciousness. Most persons think of the eyes as revealing the minds of others.

Köhler (1933) believes that the analogous conclusion hypothesis arose because of a conviction that subjective experience must be extremely different from the external bodily changes observed as behavior, and not even comparable with them. As seen by Köhler the relationship is in reality an intimate one. The visible behavior of other human beings is closely connected with their mental states and offers an immediate basis for comprehension. Examples of such observable behavior are retreating, leaning toward an object or warding it off, and assuming a tense position.

Köhler states that "All the forms of dynamic development in subjective experience can be expressed in the related forms of visible processes which occur in the perceptual field of the observer" (1933). There is no haphazard bond between affect and bodily expression. Rather, there is an orderly connection in true character. This argument removes the second prop from the empirical theory.

Are there other comprehensible relationships, in addition to understanding the subjective experience of other individuals? Can a distinction be made between incomprehensible and comprehensible connections? These questions require discussion.

When a color contrasts with another color, this fact can be *explained* causally. But, as Erismann (1924) points out, it cannot be *understood* on the basis of the internal relationship of the two colors. The same holds true for many connections established between sense impressions. Any number of connections which depend on superficial bonds can merely be noted as facts but cannot be understood.

It is not in the nature of a chair to be red; it might just as well be green. The relationship between a table and the English word, *table,* is no more comprehensible than its connection with the Latin word, *mensa.*

It is quite another matter if one drinks a refreshing glass of water, becomes angry at some one, or ascertains the reason for which a man rescued himself from an unhappy marriage by obtaining a divorce. These examples are consequences of mental processes which can later be relived. It may be stated as a principle that those mental processes which can be relived can also be understood. On this basis the connection between personal attitudes and their external effects becomes understandable. If, for instance, the wish to move an arm is followed by an arm movement, that sequence is comprehensible.

Hume was of a different opinion, and the positivists concurred with him. Hume denied that there was anything more than a purely chance sequence between an act of will and its external consequences. The association psychologists, whether positivists or of other convictions, joined with Hume in this viewpoint. Association psychology regarded comprehensibility and meaningfulness as nothing more than associative familiarity. Meaningless mental content was simply unfamiliar. Comprehensible, meaningful connections arose through repeated binding together of material that was not previously bound together. With these conclusions the older psychology believed it had solved the problem of meaning. At that time no one had begun to toil over phenomenological subtleties.

For some of us today phenomenological enlightenment is the greatest of all psychological virtues. And the phenomenological method forces us to the conclusion that hundreds of sequences of two elements in consciousness do not necessarily produce understandable connections. We also conclude that certain other mental processes can be comprehensible and meaningful at their very first contact with each other.

For the moment there seems to be no way of avoiding the distinction between understanding and explaining as it has been portrayed in preceding paragraphs. Gestalt psychology is now attempting to solve the problem. Its effort is based on the belief that a schism in the entire psychological field is unnecessary, and that it will suffice to distinguish between two categories of concepts, the descriptive and the functional.

Descriptive concepts are subjective, while functional concepts relate to the explanation of objective events. Previously the only descriptive concepts connected with each other were those which represented meaningless elements or their combinations. According to Gestalt psychology the coherence of form is not due to chance. It is determined functionally as well as phenomenologically.

Meaning, as seen from the Gestalt viewpoint, is internal form arrangement. Wertheimer states that the structure of a perceptual field arises originally because of its tendency "to become meaningful and unitary, and to be dominated by internal necessity." The Gestalt view is that anything which is not a form, but which can be thought of as simply connected by "and," is devoid of meaning. Thus meaning and meaningful processes are considered to be on the same plane, and a distinction is made between coherence of parts based on internal necessity and mere superficial coexistence.

Meaning is assumed to be inherent in form itself, and is conceded a degree of independent existence. Meaningfulness is bound up with the form factor in a way which aims to unite objective occurrence and subjective interpretation. The Gestalt approach to this problem is an effort to bridge the gap between explanation and understanding.

The writer joins Scheerer in his opposition to Gestalt psychology's endeavor to apply its one-sided viewpoint in such a way as to unify understanding and explanation in the form factor. They may not be placed on the same plane.

Scheerer (1931) states that: "Pregnance does not determine meaning; rather it is pregnance which exists because of meaning."

The actual realm of meaningful mental connections is not to be sought on the level of sensory psychology, but at a higher level, above all where motivational bonds exist. It is impossible to agree that anything which is bound together by a mere "and" must of necessity be devoid of meaning. To the janitor a pile of books on a scholar's desk may seem merely "*and*-connected," but for the researcher himself the situation is meaningful. The artistic arrangement of objects in a picture may seem merely summative to the layman. In the eyes of a connoisseur it may have deep symbolic significance. The question of whether or not a phenomenon is meaningful can by no means be settled in the peripheral stratum of perception.

CHAPTER 18

THE PSYCHOLOGY OF THINKING

It is Koffka's (1935) view that study of the thought process provides the most profound insight into the nature of holistic tendencies. Thinking, he states, is a form process governed by the same laws that apply to sensation. He suggests an analogy between the pregnance tendency towards closure of an open visual figure and closure of an "open question" as a thought form. Productive thinking, based on restructuring of thought content, is thus seen as analogous to restructuring a visual figure.

The Gestalt approach to thinking may be illustrated by picturing an individual who is on the verge of solving a technical problem. Since he lacks the most suitable tool for his purpose he looks about to see if he can improvise one. If there is no hammer to drive a nail, a pair of pliers can be used in its place. If there is no pair of pliers and the individual is resourceful he may take off a shoe and use that. To do this, naturally, he must temporarily put aside the concept of a shoe as an article of apparel and recognize its value as a hard surface for hammering. Briefly, he must restructure the object to realize its usefulness for a new purpose.

Köhler's (1925) classic experiments with chimpanzees supply another example of restructuring thought content. Motivated by a strong need, they restructured a neutral object, a branch, to form a "new" instrument for pulling fruit toward them.

Wertheimer (1925, page 176) collected many instances of productive thinking by humans. Two of these are described below:

Figure 22 shows a square with an elongated parallelogram on it. The problem is to find the sum of the areas of the square and the parallelogram. It would be possible to proceed by adding a^2 and the area of the parallelogram, $a(b-a)$. But this method is prohibited. Then, according to Wertheimer, one may hit

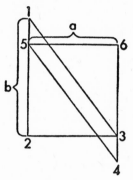

Figure 22

upon the idea of considering the figure as composed of two triangles, *1-2-3* and *4-5-6*. Their combined area is two times one half the base times the height, or $a \cdot b$. Restructuring the figure in this way makes the problem simple.

The second example is a familiar one in geometry. The subject is required to calculate the area of a circle by restructuring the circle to form a polygon with an infinite number of sides.

Wertheimer approached restructuring of material in productive thinking in still another way, by studying Barbara's method in scholastic logic. Consider this syllogism:

> All men are mortal.
> Caius is a man.
> Therefore Caius is mortal.

As seen by Wertheimer, the mere simultaneous presence of two premises does not produce a conclusion if genuinely new knowledge is sought. First the two premises must "interlock" with each other. There must be a reorientation of the facts involved. The process of arriving at a conclusion requires reorientation of the component concepts so that they will be in closer agreement with reality. This occurs in productive thinking only if a new, previously unfamiliar factor is added to the middle term.

Newton is said to have discovered the law of gravity when an apple fell from a tree. It is claimed that Galileo hit upon the law of the pendulum when he saw a chandelier swinging. But before Newton's time many had seen falling apples and before Galileo many had seen swinging chandeliers without making a revolutionary discovery. Why did the new ideas occur to just those great physicists?

Both Newton and Galileo had previously applied themselves intensively to closely related problems. Their efforts resulted in mental tension which strove towards equalization. In each instance the mental gap called for closure, and what the scientists observed just fitted into the gap like the last piece of a puzzle.

Székely (1945) has experimentally reproduced the situation of a scientist who works on a problem and solves it by reinterpreting his observations. In the first part of the experiment the subject was given three columns of watch sticks, with three sticks in each column, and three more sticks with which to work. The task he faced is illustrated in Figure 23a.

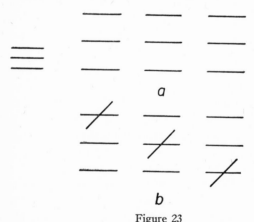

Figure 23

The task was to add the three extra sticks to the three columns in such a way that the sum of any vertical or horizontal row would be four. Few subjects succeeded in solving the prob-

lem. Those who failed to solve it were not given the correct
solution, in preparation for the second part of the experiment.
To understand Székely's procedure it is necessary to note first
that the problem can be solved by selecting a diagonal row of
sticks and placing one of the extra sticks across each stick in the
manner shown in Figure 23b.

One day later Székely's subjects were presented with another
task which apparently had no connection with the first one. A
horizontal row of lines, as pictured in Figure 24a, is shown, and
the subjects were asked to draw a perpendicular through every
third one. Figure 24b shows the task completed.

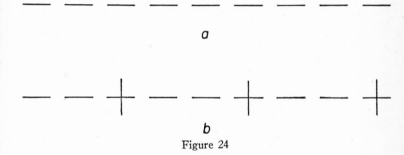

a

b

Figure 24

In the course of carrying out the second assignment, some
subjects suddenly asked for match sticks, saying they wanted
to try out an idea that had occurred to them. They then came
upon the correct solution to the first problem, as shown in Figure 23b. The unsolved problem of the previous day had left
tension. Although it was not consciously experienced, it strove
toward equilibrium and was released by the second task. The
solution of the problem reveals in miniature form the manner
in which Newton and Galileo made their epochal discoveries.

It is undoubtedly true that restructuring of material very
often constitutes one aspect of productive thinking (Duncker,
1935). But is it the most important aspect? It would appear
that the methods of Gestalt psychology cannot as yet answer
the question satisfactorily.

Scheerer (1931) offers an opinion on the outcome of Gestalt
psychology's approach to the psychology of thinking. He be-

lieves it amounts to inclusion of thinking in the realm of physical forms, and an attempt to explain it by applying the principles of natural science. However, it is impossible to reduce the spontaneity and activity of thinking simply to thought processes. Without the individual's goal-directed activity there would be no thinking. Furthermore, there could be no thinking without reference to individual meaning.

Scheerer believes that Gestalt psychology equates experienced logical contradiction with disturbance of balance. It equates logical conclusion with mental closure, as a result of which psychological forces reach a state of equilibrium. The principle applied by Gestalt psychology is supposed to possess subjective reality, logical objectivity, and physical actuality into the bargain. Surely this is an abuse of symbols.

CHAPTER 19

THE NATURE OF GESTALT PSYCHOLOGY

If it were possible to produce a systematic description of all mental life on the basis of Gestalt's psychology, a book such as the present one might begin with a definition of the fundamental concept, "Gestalt." Then, in an effort to supply an introduction to Gestalt theory it could proceed to outline the most important effects of that concept in developing a new psychology.

It is difficult to state precisely how much the leading Gestalt psychologists themselves believe they have accomplished in building their system. In the writer's opinion, with all due respect for what has already been done, a systematic portrayal of human behavior from the Gestalt viewpoint is not yet possible. On this account it seemed preferable to postpone definition of the Gestalt concept and begin instead by describing the manner in which Gestalt psychology deals with various specific problems. With that background established an endeavor can be made to clarify the Gestalt concept itself and to throw light on the nature of the new psychology from other angles.

It appears logical to begin by noting six definitions which occur in the literature of the Gestalt concept:

1. Köhler (1933) states that "Gestalt means a separate whole." With reference to the field concept he offers this observation: "Whenever a process becomes dynamically distributed and arranges itself in accordance with the constellation of determining circumstances in its entire field, that process belongs in the realm of Gestalt psychology."

2. Wertheimer's statement reads in this manner: "A Gestalt is a whole whose characteristics are determined, not by the characteristics of its individual elements, but by the internal nature of the whole."

Wertheimer contrasts a Gestalt with a sum, which he describes as follows: "A collection is a sum of parts or pieces when, and only when, it can be created by putting them together one after the other without effecting a change in the qualities of any one of them. For instance, a room can be emptied or filled piece by piece without changing any of the remaining pieces."

3. Koffka's (1935) definition resembles Köhler's, but adds a reference to the pregnance concept. He states that: "Organization is the process that leads to a Gestalt. The definition would be unsatisfactory if it failed to specify that the organization must be in accord with the law of pregnance. Organization is diametrically opposed to chance distribution."

The first three formulations are the words of the three leading Gestalt psychologists. We proceed to others:

4. Matthaei's (1929) definition is similar to those already mentioned: "The whole and the parts mutually determine the structural coherence of a Gestalt. The parts are dependently related to the whole, but they affect its organization."

5. Petermann (1929) restricts the Gestalt concept to perception: "A Gestalt is a lesser whole in the total perceptual field."

6. Sander (1926) refers to the articulation of forms in the more inclusive total consciousness: "A Gestalt is a lesser whole in the encompassing total consciousness. It is characterized by isolation and separation of its parts."

The six definitions of Gestalt psychology reveal significant features of the Gestalt concept. To begin with, they promptly reject atomistic, associationist, mechanical, and reflexological attitudes. In their dependence on phenomenology they reject behaviorism. They make the assertion that positivism cannot explain much that lies beyond what is purely factual; an example would be the meaningful nature of mental processes.

In its opposition to vitalism Köhler's theory of physical forms is an attempt to explain organic order with the same principles that apply to inorganic phenomena. The thinking of the older psychologists was static. Gestalt psychologists share with others the view that activity in mental processes presupposes sources of energy just as it does in physical processes. Their thinking is along dynamic lines.

What remains to be said about the nature of Gestalt psychology borders on epistemology and metaphysics.

Agreement with Koffka's (1935) last comprehensive portrayal of Gestalt psychology brings with it certain consequences. As he stated the matter, Gestalt psychology is trying "to explain the most complex processes which civilization creates with concepts which also apply to the simplest processes, as exemplified by the movements of electrons and protons in a single atom. It tries to accomplish this without in any way destroying the distinction between the two types of processes." Koffka also expressed the thought in this manner: "The great realms of nature, life, and the soul meet in psychology. More specifically, they meet in the central nervous system."

What is Koffka's purpose? Unmistakably he reveals an emphasis on monism, or, to use a less metaphysical term, the single-minded tendency of Gestalt psychology. Monism could hardly be emphasized more strongly. In the present context it represents a search for the material basis of all cosmic phenomena. This material basis would account for all inorganic, biopsychological, and mental processes; the last-named category would include civilization and its works. It cannot be said that the undertaking lacks boldness. The question is whether or not it can be carried out.

The pillar of the desired monistic system, that on which everything depends, is the Gestalt. More precisely, it is the physical form. Physics would become the all-embracing basic science, for psychology as well as other fields. Köhler is in accord with these views in so far as he has at times ascribed a sort of quasi-apriority to insight into physical forms. It is easy to understand why Gestalt psychology, or at least Gestalt theory, has occasionally been described as a physical discipline. In some instances the designation has simply been an objective characterization, whereas in others it implied a critical attitude.

Köhler's isomorphism may be regarded as a special sort of psychophysical parallelism. But if it should be considered possible to reduce mental phenomena to physical terms, with the physical form as the irreducible element, then mental phenomena will simply be sacrificed to monism. However, Köhler's often-repeated comments on subjective phenomena suggest that he does not in reality wish to make Gestalt psychology a physical science. He states that these subjective phenomena are the soundest reality with which psychology deals, and this train of thought does not lead to physical monism. It leans towards psychophysical parallelism, whose profundity has been increased by Gestalt theory.

It is impossible to agree completely with Koffka's view that the gulf between inorganic and biopsychological processes has been spanned. It is equally impossible to agree that a satisfactory explanation has been applied to the relationship between the mental on the one hand, and intellect as expressed in civilization, on the other.

At this point it should be reiterated that thinking cannot be explained in purely physical terms. Thought with scientific content, such as mathematical symbols, cannot be reduced to physical forms or traced back to them. Once more an emphatic warning should be sounded against a form of psychology which, with its unwarranted epistemological contentions, has done so much to delay recognition of the truly justifiable claims of the science.

CHAPTER 20

THE GESTALT PSYCHOLOGY OF MEMORY

The term "memory" first brings to mind learning, recall, and reproduction, although comparison and recognition are equally dependent upon it. Gestalt psychology has examined all of these processes. The theory of physical forms has led Gestalt psychologists to devote a considerable amount of attention to the physiological concomitants of memory phenomena, whereas the older psychologists took little notice of that aspect of the problem.

Regardless of how the theory of association and reproduction of images may have been constituted in its details, the older psychology agreed on the hypothesis that contiguity of two mental elements in space and time was enough to bind them together. Subsequent presentation of one element would then tend to recall the other.

Gestalt psychology has actively criticized the associationist view of memory. It has called attention to the fact that contiguity of mental elements in time and space does not, of itself, guarantee their association and does not insure their mutual recall.

A sort of "mental energy" is needed to produce association and recall. Gestalt terminology would refer to a need or an interest. Associative binding by contiguity of elements would be just as ineffectual as the coupling of two railroad cars which were being shunted about and happened to touch each other. Recall of one element by another cannot occur without special mental energy any more than the railroad car can move without being attached to a locomotive.

In the classic experiments on learning nonsense syllables the subject's intent to learn was taken for granted and therefore not properly evaluated. The motivation was supplied by their desire to help the experimenter, and by their interest in the activity. In experiments precisely directed at this problem it was discovered that the same material could be presented to a subject hundreds of times without the slightest effect on learning if he lacked the intent to learn. It is primarily intent to learn that causes the presented material to be organized. Organization in this sense refers to structuring or restructuring the material. Gestalt psychology readily grants that nearness in time and space has a bearing on so-called association, but only because nearness favors organization into a form.

Köhler states: "Where strong organization occurs naturally, association probably exists of its own accord. Where no true organization is already present, it is accomplished only if the individual purposefully structures the material. When the units of a series have been associated they acquire specific characteristics which depend on their position in the encompassing whole, as is the case with notes in a melody form" (1930, page 184).

The newer interpretation of learning as a structuring process has led Gestalt psychology to drop the association concept almost entirely. A number of facts can now be explained in a manner which places the older psychology in an awkward position. Two examples will be cited:

Nagel (1912) had his subjects learn series of syllables so well that they could be repeated without error. Remarkably enough, the subjects could not carry out an apparently easier task. When one syllable of a series was presented at random they were unable to recall the syllable that came after it. For Gestalt psychology the explanation is simple. The separate syllables had been removed from their form combinations and as a result had acquired entirely different characteristics.

The second illustration, taken from ordinary experience, can be explained in a similar manner. It is very difficult to separate one fragmentary movement of a dance or other combination of movements and execute it by itself.

It has been claimed that meaningful words are easier to associate because they have previously been combined with other elements. In opposition to this view Köhler (1933, page 182) states that if a word combination such as phosphorus-Minerva or strychnin-golf is chosen, it is impossible to say they have ever been connected. Nevertheless, if they do combine more readily it is probably because of the amusing connotations they suggest. In some noteworthy experiments conducted with his students, Köhler investigated nonsense syllables, the favorite material of association psychology. He showed that the difficulty of learning nonsense syllables may be attributed to their extreme monotony. It is primarily this monotonous quality, rather than their lack of meaning, which makes it so hard to structure nonsense syllables.

Another memory problem is the experience of recognition. It is an everyday occurrence to recognize a person one has already met. The impression may be that he has changed considerably in the meantime. In such instances there is a temptation to assume the existence of a mental image of the individual's previous appearance. Careful introspection, however, refutes this hypothesis. No independent image is required when an earlier impression is compared with a present one. Recognition and comparison are made possible because of exact equivalents of the previous impressions in the central nervous system. These equivalents are the "traces." The form of the original experience corresponds to the form of the neurological trace which is retained.

If an ambiguous figure is seen only in one of its possible forms, "A," but not in its alternate form, "B," it will subsequently be recognized only if it is again seen as "A." If a vase is seen in Figure 14, page 47, rather than two faces, future recognition depends on seeing it again as a vase. Yet the actual retinal image is the same in either case. The retinal image as such leaves no trace. The trace is determined by the manner in which the figure is experienced.

A second example of the manner in which a trace is established is recognition of a tune when it is played in a different key. Such recognition is evidence that the trace of the tune form is operating, rather than the traces of the individual notes as they impinged on the sound receptors. Again it is the individual's impression which is retained rather than the simple sense data.

Another Gestalt critique based on organized memory units deals with recall. According to the older view a sufficient part of a whole previously impressed on memory should readily recall

that original whole. The drawing ⊔ should recall an "H"

since from an atomistic viewpoint only a small portion of the familiar letter is missing. However, if the experiment is conducted with unbiased subjects the anticipated recall usually fails to occur. Gestalt psychology correctly explains the negative result by pointing out that the experiment actually deals with two essentially different forms. The well-known letter was previously experienced, but the second form is new and is presented currently for the first time.

Figure 25 will provide additional evidence for the Gestalt

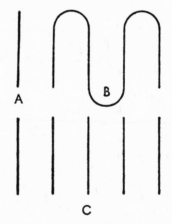

Figure 25

view. The subject is shown line "A" together with the serpentine line "B." Later it can be established that "A" alone will recall "B" most effectively. The five-lined figure "C," when shown alone, is not nearly as effective in recalling "B." This is noteworthy because "C," in an atomistic, summative sense contains much more of the original "A" plus "B" than does "A" by itself. The older psychology would have expected the recall value of "C" to be greater.

Among the classic experiments of older memory research are those concerned with so-called inhibitions. Only studies dealing with association and recall will be referred to here.

A simple description shows clearly what is meant by associative inhibition. If syllable "a" has already been associated with syllable "b," then syllable "a" will not become associated with a new syllable, "c," as readily as would be the case if "a" had not previously been linked with "b." However, if "a" has been associated with both "b" and "c" at approximately the same time, the result is associative inhibition. There is conflict between "b" and "c" for preference in recall as a response to "a" presented alone. Either may be recalled with some delay or there may be an instance of so-called contamination which is really a mixture of "b" and "c." The competition between "b" and "c" would be an example of inhibited recall.

One of Karl Bühler's pupils, Frings (1914), has shown that under certain circumstances memory inhibitions disappear completely. Series of syllables were memorized in groups of three such as "a-b-c," "d-e-f," etc. The groups were recited as anapests, i.e., with less emphasis on the first two letters of each group and an accent on the last. If two groups were "a-b-c" and "d-b-e," it is clear that the older psychology would anticipate inhibition with respect to recall of "c" and "e" since both had been connected with "b." Actually no such inhibition occurred. This outcome is understandable in the light of Gestalt psychology, for "b" is regarded merely as a component part, in one instance in the unit "a-b-c," and in the other instance in the unit "d-b-e." On one occasion "c" and at another time "e" was a part of those units. There is no such thing as an identical part "b," of and by itself, in the two groupings of letters.

Lewin (1935) showed the extent to which recall depends on the characteristics of the original learning situation. His work emphasized the holistic nature of learning.

In an experiment a series of syllables was memorized so thoroughly that it could easily be recited. When the subject was subsequently shown a single syllable taken from the series, but was not instructed to recall the syllables which followed it, as a rule they did not occur to him. According to the older viewpoint they should have come to mind because the strength of the association was considered the only important factor in recall. In the procedure described the associations were particularly well established.

Gestalt psychology has no difficulty in explaining the result just noted. Even the closest bond will not suffice for recall. Recall depends far more on other attendant circumstances, among which the structuring of the total situation would ordinarily be outstanding. The total situation when the syllable series was recited was completely different from the total situation when selected single syllables were presented. Familiarity, of and by itself, signifies nothing. It appears to advantage only when there is a need or intent which can make use of the opportunity.

In an abstracted state an individual may be temporarily unaware of the needs that are usually active, and habitual, automatic behavior may come into play. He may be surprised to find himself slipping into behavior that is not at all wanted at the time. Those whose occupations require them to perform many routine tasks are particularly subject to this tendency. It gives rise to the typical bureaucrat.

The concept of perseveration had considerable significance for the older psychology. The term applies to images which do not enter consciousness in the usual associative manner, but occur without obvious stimulus. The older psychologists said little about the processes underlying perseveration. Gestalt psychology, on the other hand, with its dynamic approach, has attempted to solve the problem.

Köhler (1933) interprets perseveration of a planned activity as the effect of tension which operates until it is released. Zeigarnik (1927) carried out experiments which produced new insight into the tension conditions which arise when projects are interrupted. His subjects were required to solve a series of problems of approximately equal difficulty and interest. They were allowed to complete only some of the tasks, while the others were interrupted. The number of completed and uncompleted tasks was equal. Afterwards the subjects were asked to list all the tasks they had undertaken. The results showed that on the average a substantially larger number of uncompleted tasks were recalled.

Zeigarnik's experimental results are explained in this way: A subject who attempts to solve a problem enters into a state of tension which is usually released only when a solution is reached. The first step in bringing a task to a conclusion is to picture the conclusion mentally. It is easy to understand why uncompleted tasks are better recalled than those which are carried to completion.

The difference between the memory value of completed and unfinished assignments becomes smaller in the course of time. Apparently the tension is gradually released.

CHAPTER 21

GESTALT LAWS OF MENTAL WORK

Kraepelin (1902) was the first to study work with the techniques of experimental psychology. In one investigation he required his subjects to add one-place integers for a considerable length of time—usually an hour—and noted how many problems they solved. Each problem consisted of only two numbers to be added; the sum was not to be placed under the two addends, but to the right of them. Every integer was used twice because the second addend of one problem appeared again as the first addend in the next problem.

The subjects were instructed to draw a line every time a stop signal was given, so that it would be possible to trace in detail the structuring of productivity during the period of the experiment. The work periods usually were three minutes in length, but at times they were reduced to one minute.*

Kraepelin's findings showed that exceptionally rapid workers completed more than 4,000 sums in an hour. Thus each single addition required less than one second.

As explained by Kraepelin, the form of the work curve was determined by a number of factors, some facilitating the work process and others inhibiting it. Among them were practice, fatigue, and habituation, the latter accompanied by the release of all varieties of incidental imagery. Another factor was incentive, which combats a condition that may be compared with the inertia of physical masses; it should be noted that both the beginning and ending of a movement are difficult. Lastly, there were factors connected with will, the most noteworthy being initial spurt, distraction, and final spurt of energy.

* More recently Läpple (1942) made use of work periods lasting forty seconds. However, experiments conducted since Kraepelin's have not produced adequate accounts of how productivity is structured in shorter work periods.

Kraepelin realized, of course, that addition of two numbers such as 3 and 5, 7 and 8, and so on, is the simplest, most mechanical sort of calculation. In fact he strove for just such an automatic work process because it seemed to offer him the best assurance that he would obtain intellectual work in a "pure" form. It is apparent that in holding this belief he was governed by the atomistic psychological attitudes of his time. Kraepelin's problems in addition correspond to the nonsense syllables of the older memory studies, and the mechanically executed additions correspond to pure associations, devoid of meaning.

There was another element which did even more to atomize the work process in Kraepelin's experiments and those of Pauli (1943), who followed his example. It was the fact that the material to be added was presented in as disorganized a manner as the technique of printing or writing would permit. In some experiments the work sheets contained as many as 2,000 numbers arranged in 40 columns of 50 numbers each. These suggested as forcefully as possible to the subject that he was dealing with formless material.

What is the purpose of measures which serve to destroy all subtle qualitative variations in the work process? Why should there be such excessive atomizing, produced by the external arrangement of material? Apparently it was hoped that such conditions would result in a work curve approaching as closely as possible the true nature of an automatic process. Unfortunately certain drives add their practically uncontrollable influences to the subject's will tension, which, it is assumed, remains constant. They cause the work curve to rise and fall. The uncontrollable nature of these drives is shown by the strikingly small amount of agreement among individual work curves.

The Kraepelinian method served to eliminate all original formative forces implicit in intellectual work, as well as all specific plans of action. Since it was found impossible to control these factors directly, an attempt was made to by-pass them by monotonous structuring of the work process and formless arrangement of the material.

Analogy with the psychology of perception throws light on Kraepelin's procedures. It was as if his subjects had been required to observe their subjective visual gray and note changes in the course of one hour, or to listen to the same pitch for the same length of time and note changes in subjective oscillation.

The writer's experiments have shown that formative work forces can be mobilized largely of their own accord even in Kraepelin's procedures, simply by altering the external arrangement of the material in an appropriate way (Katz, 1946).

It is surprising that the Gestalt psychologists have missed the opportunity of studying the work curve. In spite of their resourcefulness in discovering concepts to criticize, they overlooked that segment of atomistic psychology. Pure sensation is merely a borderline case of natural perception. Mechanical association is a borderline case of genuine thinking, and the automatic course of a reaction is a borderline case of voluntary action. It is equally true that continuous addition of paired numbers, carried out with unstructured material, is nothing more than a borderline case of intellectual work. Only assembly line activity of the most monotonous sort—with which industry in Kraepelin's time was not yet blessed—is related to automatic methods of investigating work. Even in that case the similarity is superficial.

The foregoing critique is aimed only at Kraepelin's concept of the nature of intellectual work and the consequences of that concept. Beyond a doubt the factors analyzed by the noted scientist can have an effect on the course of mental activity.

Genuine work processes are goal-directed, meaningful, and have the characteristics of structured wholes. Their segmental acts, or components, are so interrelated that the correctness of the entire result is endangered if an error is made in any part of the task. Natural work projects do not ordinarily occupy extremely short periods of time, as did Kraepelin's addition problems. It will be recalled that they required approximately one second or even less.

Problems in addition can be well suited to realistic investigations of mental work if they are structured with wider scope than Kraepelin granted them in his two-figure units. They must be organized in such a way that the distinguishing characteristics of genuine work processes—mentioned above—can come into play. The writer recently conducted experiments which aimed at fulfilling these requirements, and the results demonstrate new principles of mental work. The conclusions may be summarized as follows:

In any given type of task, the details of the work process—such as its progress and reliability—are determined by the nature of the total task of which they are parts.

It seems justifiable to offer the conclusion as a Gestalt law of mental work. In view of its wide scope it might be designated as the basic principle governing the structuring of such activity. It is obviously similar to the most inclusive Gestalt law governing perception, which states that the impressions made by the parts of a form are determined by the whole.

The parallel between the psychology of perception and the psychology of mental work is not limited to one general Gestalt law. It is always possible to discover certain analogies with other bodies of knowledge even if they are not closely related. However, the structural similarities between perception and the work process are based on more than a vague analogy. It can be shown that strong and weak work forms correspond to strong and weak perceptual forms, and that disintegration of forms in both areas occurs in analogous circumstances. Furthermore, close grouping of different work forms does not result in their fusion, any more than it does in the case of perceptual forms. In other words, the law of the "good" curve, or common destiny, also applies to work forms. Naturally the correspondence between principles applying to the work process and those governing perceptual forms is not perfect. Perfect agreement could hardly be expected, since perceptual processes also occur in the course of passive behavior, while even the simplest work processes require active goal setting and execution.

Following are accounts of seven experiments designed to clarify the nature of mental work:

Experiment 1. Subjects were required to add columns of 20 one-digit, two-digit, and three-digit numbers. The integers used ranged from 1 to 9, and their sequence was left to chance.

It should be noted that in the addition of numbers with more than one digit, a remainder must be carried to the tens column, and from there a remainder must be carried to the hundreds column, thus in effect increasing the numbers to be added in those columns from 20 to 21. To compensate for this fact and equalize the addition task for each column, one more integer was added at the top of each units column, i.e., the column at the extreme right. A sample, shown below, will make clear the arrangement of the work sheets. For the sake of brevity, 5 and 6 addends are presented instead of 20 and 21 :

One-Digit Numbers	Two-Digit Numbers		Three-Digit Numbers		
Units	Tens	Units	Hundreds	Tens	Units
8		9			4
4	3	5	3	5	9
9	9	3	4	7	5
3	2	7	2	9	7
7	8	4	5	6	2
6	6	8	8	3	3
—	—	—	—	—	—

The instructions were to add the columns as quickly as possible, without error. Work was timed with a stop watch to $\frac{1}{5}$ second accuracy, calculated without the time taken to write down answers and carry over remainders. For this reason all time intervals referred to will cover only the actual work of addition.

It might be anticipated that the time required to add the units columns of 21 addends would be the same whether those columns were in the one-digit, two-digit, or three-digit problems. One would not expect a later event to have a retroactive effect on the addition process. The same percentage of errors would be anticipated in the three instances mentioned.

From the standpoint of atomistic psychology it would be expected that the time required for the units columns, for the tens columns in the two-digit problems, and the hundreds columns in the three-digit problems, would be approximately the same. The isolated task of adding any column would appear to be equal to the task of adding any other isolated column of similar length. One would also expect the number of errors to show little variation. Actually none of the expectations mentioned was verified. Table 1 shows average values for 10 subjects:

TABLE 1

TIME REQUIRED TO ADD COLUMNS OF ONE-DIGIT, TWO-DIGIT, AND THREE-DIGIT NUMBERS

	One-Digit Problems	Two-Digit Problems		Three-Digit Problems		
	Units Column	Units Column	Tens Column	Units Column	Tens Column	Hundreds Column
Addition time in seconds	15.2	16.3	17.1	16.7	18.1	19.
Per cent of error	22.8	14.2	16.5	7.4	14.8	24.

The findings with respect to addition time may be summed up as follows: Time for addition of the units columns increases from the one-digit problems to the three-digit problems. It took longer to add the tens columns than to add the units columns, the differences being 5 per cent and 8 per cent respectively. The addition time for the hundreds columns was somewhat greater than for the tens columns.

The table reveals these facts about errors: The percentage of errors did not remain approximately constant for the one-digit, two-digit, and three-digit problems. It decreased from 22.8 per cent in the one-digit problems to 14.2 per cent in the units column of the two-digit problems, and to only 7.4 per cent in the three-digit problems. In the two-digit and three-digit problems the percentage of errors increased from the units to the tens columns and from the tens to the hundreds.

The factors Kraepelin invoked to analyze the work curve contribute little toward understanding the results described in Table 1. No doubt practice and fatigue can take effect in work processes which last more than an hour. But they could hardly be influential when each isolated calculation requires less than a minute as a rule and seldom more than that. In the experiment reported measures were taken to neutralize the effects of practice and fatigue as much as possible. This was accomplished by alternating the order of the various tasks on successive days.

Familiarity and incentive are two other factors which do not aid in explaining the results obtained.

A factor which deserves consideration is the initial spurt of effort referred to by Kraepelin. He believed it explained the fact that in many work curves productivity in the first time unit is greater than in the second. It was possible to try to connect the initial spurt with the smaller amount of time required to add the units column in the two-place and three-digit problems, as compared with time required for the tens columns. This explanation is untenable in the light of Experiment 6, to be described shortly. It may be added that there was no sign of a final spurt in Table 1.

The correct explanation of the results of Experiment 1 must be based on holistic psychology. To begin with, there is the fact that the one-digit numbers were added more quickly than the units columns in the two-digit and three-digit problems. It may be conjectured that the burden of anticipated work on a second column, or on a second and third column, impairs work on the units column. These circumstances may seem comparable with retroactive inhibition as it appears in the classic psychology of memory, and might suggest an analogy. But the differences between the two cases should not be overlooked. They differ with respect to mental set, and the psychophysical processes which cause difficulty could be essentially unlike. Whatever the precise explanation of it may be, such inhibition in intellectual activity is a remarkable fact and one which calls for the viewpoint of holism.

Anticipation of work to be done suggests analogy with a runner's mental set toward the stretch he must cover. There is one difference, however. The runner deliberates about the distribution of his energy, but the subject in the experimental procedure begins his calculations without conscious reflection.

Retroactivity affects the units column not only by increasing the calculation time, but by influencing the reliability of the work as well. It is noteworthy that the burden of anticipated work does not lower the quality of the initial task in the experiment, but actually raises it. The average percentage of errors decreases steadily from the one-place through the two-digit and three-digit problems. Retroactive inhibition of calculation time and retroactive facilitation of reliability occur simultaneously. Without further confirmation it might be unwise to accept this apparently paradoxical result. But such confirmation has been supplied by other investigations.

Apparently the subject realizes that an error in the units column will lead to an error in the final result even if the remaining columns are correctly added. Therefore, the more columns there are to come, the more cautious he is in his efforts on the first column. For the same reason, the more columns there are to come, the more slowly he adds that first column. Far from being mutually contradictory, it is clear that retroactive inhibition of speed and facilitation of quality actually complement each other.

It seemed essential to prove conclusively that the results obtained depended in fact on the location of the columns, or, more precisely, that the external form of the addition material corresponded to the internal work form. It had to be shown that chance differences in the difficulty of the columns were not responsible for the outcome. For this reason columns were alternated in such a manner that they appeared just as frequently in each position of the one-digit, two-digit, and three-digit problems. Since some columns had 20 and others 21 addends, their identity during alternation was not absolute; however, it is clear that they differed only by one number in such instances.

Even under the circumstances outlined the operation of Gestalt principles was unmistakable. Although the elements dealt with were for all practical purposes identical, organization of the calculation task was determined by the wholes of which those elements were component parts. The analogy with perceptual phenomena is striking.

Experiment 2. What is the relationship between calculation time and the number of addends? The second experiment was designed to answer this question.

Columns of 10, 15, 20, 25, and 30 addends were arranged, each column increasing by 5 addends until a total of 60 addends had been reached. Following this series were columns which decreased, also in steps of 5 addends, from a total of 60 addends to the last column, which had a total of 10 addends.

Addition time varied with the increasing and decreasing length of the columns. It required more time per addend to add those of increasing length. Columns in the decreasing series, however, required comparatively more time per addend. Apparently the increasing sequence had a stimulating effect on work tempo, while the decreasing lengths produced inhibition.

Table 2 shows that the addition time does not increase in direct proportion to the number of addends. It increases with

TABLE 2

Time Required to Add Columns of Increasing Length

Number of addends	10	15	20	25	30	35	40	45	50	55	60
Average addition time in seconds	4.2	10.4	17.4	24.2	33.4	37.2	46.7	63.9	69.2	74.6	80.2
Time in seconds per addend	.42	.69	.87	.96	1.1	1.05	1.16	1.4	1.38	1.35	1.34

disproportionate rapidity. While the time per addend for the 10-addend columns is .42 second, it mounts to 1.34 seconds for the 60-addend columns.

There is a temptation to connect the large proportionate increase in addition time for longer columns of addends with the continually increasing size of the sums concerned. However, other investigations conducted by the writer have a bearing on this problem. They show that an approximately similar increase in average time per addend takes place as the number of problems increases, even if they are in pairs, as they were in Kraepelin's research. With materials arranged in that manner the size of the sums dealt with does not increase, and there is no feeling that the success of the whole operation depends on success in each part of it.

It seems that the varying length of the columns produces a varying set, which in turn automatically results in an appropri-

ate distribution of energy. It is true that the distribution of
energy is somewhat dependent on the relationship between one
column and the next; this was revealed by results obtained with
gradual increase in the length of the columns followed by a
gradual decrease. But that dependence may be considered an elementary phenomenon of work structuring. Experiment 1 shows
that addition time for a column varied with its location in the
whole two-place and three-place problems. Experiment 2 shows
that a similar variation in addition time takes place even when
the columns in a series seem completely independent of each other.
In the first experiment the form of the whole could be considered strong. In the second it would be termed weak, and nothing more than an *"and*-connection."

Every complex arrangement of problems tends to create a
special atmosphere for the lesser problems of which it consists,
and determines their nature. This was seen primarily in the
addition time, but was also evident in the reliability of the calculations. Another interesting example is the different periods
of time required to add columns of 20 (21) addends in Experiment 1 and those of similar length in Experiment 2. All subjects in Experiment 1 added these more quickly, with an average of 15.2 seconds. The average time for such columns in
Experiment 2 was 17.4 seconds.

Experiment 3. When subjects are asked to add two-digit
numbers, a new question may be raised. What is the proportionate length of time required to add the units columns and the
tens columns when the number of addends is varied?

Investigation proved that the relationship between the addition times for individual columns varies with their length. The
quotient of addition times for each column of two-digit problems
is largest for a problem of medium length. It decreases for
shorter and longer problems. On this basis it may be said that
the work form for medium numbers of addends is most subject
to pregnance.

Experiment 4. It is possible to "loosen" the cohesion of
visual forms by marking off the elements of which they are
composed. This forces the observer to see the elements more as

separate entities. The same holds true for acoustic forms and other varieties as well.

By means of a special arrangement of the materials, it was shown that work forms, too, can be loosened by compelling the subject to pay more attention to the individual elements, addends in this instance. The desired situation was easily created by having the addends in roman instead of the usual arabic numerals. Although roman numerals are familiar, the subject is not accustomed to adding them, and is compelled to examine them more carefully.

The investigation showed that the use of roman numerals eliminated the characteristic differences in addition time for various columns. The average time per addend remained approximately constant.

Experiment 5. Everyday experience reveals that energy expenditure is apportioned in accordance with the difficulty and duration of anticipated work. A runner in the 100-yard dash uses his strength differently from a runner in the first 100 yards of a mile run. He makes this adjustment consciously. However, as was suggested above, there are also task adjustments which come about without deliberation. They are analogous to perceptual adjustments which are made in the presence of forms which differ in complexity. Unplanned adjustments may be demonstrated indirectly by means of problems in addition.

The procedure consisted of presenting the subject with columns of numbers in such a way that he could not know their length while he worked on the problems. Only two numbers were visible, and the paper containing the remainder of the column was hidden under another paper. The subject was required to pull these remaining columns from under the shielding paper, one number at a time, as quickly as he was able to add each number to the sum already reached. As soon as he found that no more numbers appeared on the paper, he was to write down the total.

Marked differences were found in addition time per addend when the extent of work could not be seen in advance, as compared with circumstances under which such a survey was possible. However, the difference decreased rapidly with increasing numbers of addends. It ranged from a difference of 48 per cent for 10 addends to 4.5 per cent for 60 addends. The number of errors was much greater when the work could not be surveyed beforehand.

Slower calculation did not insure greater reliability. Instead, the hidden nature of the total task had the double effect of increasing calculation time and lessening reliability. Apparently work of unknown extent weakens the initial spurt of energy, even if it does not eliminate it entirely. It is only natural that the initial spurt should be absent when the subject does not know how much work he must do.

It should be noted that lessened initial energy is in keeping with the finding that the differences in addition time become smaller as the length of the task increases. At least some lessening of the final spurt of energy is also to be expected. It is likely that differences in the intermediate areas of the columns would be comparatively small.

The results suggest research with partially concealed visual forms, or forms in other modalities. To date the problem of forms as they gradually come into being has received little attention.

Experiment 6. The interpretation of several visual figures which are closely involved with each other takes place in accordance with the law of the good curve, or common destiny. The principle also applies to work forms which become enmeshed with each other. A simple example will demonstrate its operation.

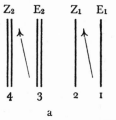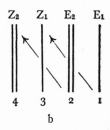

Figure 26

In Figure 26, "a" represents two two-place addition problems with units columns E_1 and E_2, as well as tens columns Z_1 and Z_2. Each column consists of 20 or 21 addends, for reasons made clear in Experiment 1. Each of the two problems is to be solved by itself.

Diagram "b" shows one of the ways in which the two addition problems can be intertwined with each other. The numbers 1–4 give the sequence in which the columns are to be added. The arrows show how the remainders must be carried in this combination of the two problems. In the experimental procedure the columns of one problem were in black, while the others were in red ink.

The question to be answered was whether the four columns in "b" would be computed in accordance with the work form of a four-place problem, or whether the two-place work form would persist. The results show plainly that the latter was the case.

As a sample, the time in seconds required by one subject to complete parts of "b" is shown below:

Units Column E_1	11.2	Tens Column Z_1	15.
Units Column E_2	11.9	Tens Column Z_2	14.8

The sample results show that the two intertwined problems were treated as if they were virtually independent of each other. If the two problems had actually fused, Column 2 would have been treated as a second column in the fused problem, and would have taken longer to add. In reality Column 2 was treated as the first column of a new problem, and took about the same length of time as the first column of the first problem, namely Column 1.

The fact that the four contiguous columns were regarded as two pairs belonging to two separate problems showed that the law of common destiny applies to work forms. Tension systems which are determined by different sets of instructions or tasks do not fuse. For at least some length of time they remain separate from each other.

Experiment 6 is of interest not only because it demonstrates the nature of form processes with particular clarity, but also because it throws more light on the results of the other experiments summarized here. To be specific, it makes it impossible to consider mere fatigue responsible for the fact that it invariably took longer to add the tens columns than to add the units columns. When later columns were added in the interlocking addition problems, there was no sign of a fatigue factor.

Experiment 7. The preceding experiments made use of abstract numbers. The following investigations were carried out to discover how addition time is affected by use of a monetary designation, with a decimal point to indicate fractions. The Swedish *krona* was chosen, but it is probable that any other currency would produce the same result.

Adhering to the one-place, two-place, and three-place arrangement of problems, the following types of addends appeared on the work sheets: 0.20 kr., 6.90 kr., and 83.50 kr.

Results are summarized in Table 3, which presents average rates for 5 subjects:

TABLE 3

AVERAGE TIME IN SECONDS FOR ADDITION OF "DENOMINATED" AND "UNDENOMINATED" NUMBERS

	One-Place Problems	Two-Place Problems		Three-Place Problems		
	Units Column	Units Column	Tens Column	Units Column	Tens Column	Hundreds Column
Undenominated	11.9	12.6	14.4	13.7	14.6	16.0
Denominated (in *krona*)	13.7	13.8	14.8	15.0	16.0	17.4

In every instance the addition time for denominated numbers was greater. The difference amounts to 1.6 seconds, or 12 per cent. It is remarkable that an obviously extraneous factor such as a monetary denomination should make the calculation task so much more difficult. However, the result is not unexpected in the light of experiments conducted by the writer in 1932, with German school children as subjects. They not only showed that the addition of a monetary designation increases the difficulty of calculation, but also that this difficulty becomes greater when, instead of a familiar denomination—the *Reichsmark,* in that case—an unfamiliar one such as the *Schilling* is substituted. It is a new finding, however, to prove that this factor is effective even with adults, who might be expected to realize that the logical calculation process is not influenced by such a superficial factor as the monetary terms attached to the numbers. The phenomenon may be termed "mental dazzle," and will be dealt with in the following chapter.

At this point it is appropriate to refer to a study of *Gestalt laws in athletic performance:*

On various occasions an individual may swim or run a distance of 60, 120, or 180 meters. The problem at hand concerns the time required for the first 60 meters of the 120- and 180-meter distances, compared with the time required for the first course, whose entire length is 60 meters. It might confidently be anticipated that there would be an increase in time for the first 60 meters as the total distance increased, but experimental verification is needed. The following report describes an investigation of running:

The subjects were 61 schoolboys between the ages of 13 and 16. The distances run were 60, 120, and 180 meters, with the finish clearly marked in the usual manner. Another condition required the subject to run a course without a marked finish; he was simply to keep on running until a stop signal was given. In reality the distance was 180 meters, but the subject was not informed of this fact. The variation represented by these circumstances corresponds to the procedure in Experiment 5, in which the subject was asked to add a series of numbers without knowing how many there would be.

Detailed arrangements for the running experiments were as follows:

Two timekeepers with stop watches were present, one to check the time for the entire distance, the other to check the time for the first 60 meters. The timekeeper at the 60-meter mark was hidden from the runner. The starting signal was given with a flag.

Findings are presented in Table 4.

TABLE 4

TIME REQUIRED TO RUN THE FIRST 60 METERS OF A COURSE UNDER
FOUR CONDITIONS

Series	Distance in Meters	Time in Seconds for Whole Course	Time in Seconds for First 60 m.	Per Cent of Increase over Series 1
1	60	9.6	9.6	..
2	120	19.4	9.8	2
3	180	31.1	10.2	6
4	180 (Unmarked)	33.4	10.8	13

The time for the first 60 meters increases with the length
of the entire course. The increase is seen to be 2 per cent from
the 60- to the 120-meter course, 6 per cent from the 60- to the
180-meter course, and when the runner has to run for an un-
defined length of time over an unmarked course, the difference
mounts to 13 per cent. The changes in Series 2 and 3 are
small, and might seem insignificant if it were not for the fact
that an increase occurred in almost every case. In one instance
the time for the first 60 meters of the 120-meter course decreased by about 1 per cent; in 5 instances it remained the same;
in 56 cases the increases ranged from 1 per cent to 7 per cent.
The time for the first 60 meters of the 180-meter course was
unchanged twice, and rose by approximately 1 per cent to 19
per cent in 59 cases. In Series 4, the last condition, the time
for the first 60 meters was greater in all 61 cases, and the increases ranged from 2 per cent to 35 per cent.

In summary it may be stated that although the increase in
running time from Series 1 to Series 2 was not large, it occurred with astonishing regularity. The small size of this
increase from Series 1 to Series 2 makes it most unlikely that
the runners intentionally reduced their speed for the first 60
meters of the 120-meter course. It appears probable that in
both series the subject concentrated on maximum speed and
that the main reason, if not the only one, for the greater speed
over the 60-meter course is the inclusion of the final spurt of
energy.

CHAPTER 22

CONNECTIVE INHIBITION AND MENTAL DAZZLE IN THOUGHT PROCESSES

The preceding chapter demonstrated retroactive inhibition in thought processes such as simple arithmetic calculations. The findings now to be presented are evidence that calculation also involves proactive inhibition, as the term is used in the psychology of memory. It will be shown that strong mutual inhibition occurs between the simple mental processes which play a part in a unitary task. The writer's experiments, which have led to the discovery of these "connective inhibitions," also contribute new data on the restructuring of mental tasks (Katz, 1949).

All experiments with adult subjects made use of numbers from 1 to 9, each of which was separately written on one of 9 square cards. In the case of children the arrangement was similar except for the fact that the numbers ranged only from 1 to 5, and were separately written on 5 cards. The simplification of the problems which resulted from this restriction of numbers permitted the children to complete their tasks in the same time required by adults for their greater range of numbers, thus neutralizing the effect of age differences.

The reports cover seven different basic experiments, each of which required a short time. But a new subject had to be used for each task, because the experience "spoils" him for the next procedure. For this reason even a small number of basic experiments necessitated a large number of subjects to obtain reliable statistical results.

It should be understood without reiteration that throughout the experimental series 9 cards were used for adults and 5 cards for children.

Procedure 1. The subject is seated at a table and the cards are placed on it. They are arranged one above the other, in the order 1, 2, 3 . . . 9 (or 1, 2 . . . 5). The experimenter asks: "What is the sum of these numbers?" As soon as he has asked the question he starts a stop watch, and stops it when the subject answers. If the answer is wrong it is rejected and the timing is continued until the correct answer is given. All time records are for correct solutions.

Procedure 2. The cards are placed on the table in an irregular order, 7, 6, 1, 2, 8, 5, 9, 4, 3 for adults, and 4, 1, 2, 5, 3 for children. Instructions and other details are the same as in Procedure 1.

Procedure 3. The experimenter holds the cards in his hands like playing cards. Again they are in an increasing order, so that the entire "1" can be seen, but the other numbers are only partly visible. The experimenter says: "I have the numbers 1 to 9 in my hand." He then folds the cards together into a pack and continues: "What sum do you get when you add all these numbers?"

Procedure 4. The experimenter holds the cards in his hand as he did in Procedure 3, and says: "I have the numbers 1 to 9 in my hand." He then continues: "Now I put the cards in a box and shake them." He performs this act, and asks: "Do you understand? Now if I were to take all the numbers out of the box, write them down, and add them, how much would I have?"

Procedure 5. The experimenter acts as he did in Procedure 4, until he has asked, "Do you understand?" He continues with: "I take all the numbers out of the box and write them down. When I have done that I put them back, shake them, take them out again, and write them down with the others. How much do I have if I add all the numbers I have written down?" In this way Procedure 4 is carried out twice in succession.

Procedure 6. The experimenter acts as he did in Procedure 4, until he has asked, "Do you understand?" But he continues with: "I take all the numbers out of the box and write them down. When I have done that I put them back, shake them, take just one number out and write it down with the others.

What is the *largest* possible sum I could get by adding all the numbers I have written down?"

Procedure 7. (*Variation of "6"*). The experimenter acts as he did in Procedure 6. But he concludes with: "What is the *smallest* possible sum I could get by adding all the numbers I have written down?"

It need hardly be said that adults had no difficulty whatsoever in understanding instructions for the various procedures. The same may be said for the majority of the children. In their case the experimenter attempted to make comprehension as easy as possible by means of slow speech, proper emphasis, and appropriate gestures. These comments would be superfluous if it were not for the fact that at least some of the results, on first impression, seem so paradoxical that there might be some doubt as to whether or not the subjects had actually understood the instructions.

The children's group consisted of 224 pupils from 10 to 14 years of age, approximately half boys and half girls. They were about equally distributed among elementary grades 3 to 7.* Every procedure was carried out with 32 pupils. Since each subject could be used for only one of the seven procedures, the attainment of comparable results necessitated matching the seven groups of subjects as closely as possible with respect to age, intelligence, and arithmetic skill. On this basis there is good reason for attributing the findings to the nature of the various calculation tasks.

The adult groups were smaller. Two procedures included 8 subjects, two had 7, another two had 6, and one less significant procedure, the second, had 4. The statistics for adults, considered by themselves, are not as satisfactory as might be desired. Nevertheless the differences in the various procedures were so large, and so much in agreement with results of the children's groups, that they may be considered reliable.

Table 5 presents the findings.

The discussion will not dwell on errors in calculation, an interesting aspect in its own right. It may be pointed out,

---

* *Volksschule.*

TABLE 5

AVERAGE CALCULATION TIME FOR SEVEN PROCEDURES

Procedure	Time in Seconds	
	Children	Adults
1	6.3	7.2
2	10.1	10.
3	27.6	18.
4	37.6	21.1
5	67.7	85.1
6	78.1	56.3
7	113.4	54.4

nevertheless, that they increased with the difficulty of the task. The last three procedures could not be carried out by all the children, and many adults succeeded in them only after several mistakes.

Subjects were always questioned about the manner in which they solved the problems. Methods varied considerably, and five reports by pupils will serve as examples:

a. Addition from the top down. As might be expected, this was the most popular approach, accounting for about half of the reports.

b. Addition from the bottom up. This method accounted for about a third of the reports. Its frequency might be due partly to the fact that the bottom-most number was nearest to the subject. When small-size numbers are written on paper— instead of being presented on cards—the bottom-to-top method declines to a small percentage.

c. Approximately a tenth of the subjects regrouped the numbers by using the method with which young Karl Friedrich Gauss was said to have astounded his school teacher; he had grouped the numbers from 1 to 9 four times and added 5 to the 40 obtained in that manner. Our pupils added 1 plus 4, 2 plus 3, thus obtaining 10, and added the remainder of 5. The number of pupils who hit upon the Gaussian solution is surprisingly large, and considerably greater than the number of adults who spontaneously thought of it.

d. About 4 per cent resorted to "semi-grouping," in which they combined only two numbers in the manner described in "c," and added the others without special arrangement.

e. There remain those subjects who combined the numbers in an order different from their actual presentation in the experiments, but who followed no systematic method in doing so. They were unable to account for their unsystematic approach. Procedures 5, 6, and 7, which involve two steps, produced a great variety of other addition methods whose details need not be of further concern in the present context.

Results as shown in the table may be summarized in this way:

Timing in Procedure 1 can be considered normal for both adults and children. With the shift from an ordered series in Procedure 1 to the random presentation of Procedure 2, there is an approximately equal increase in time for both categories; it is not unexpectedly large.

Comparison of the outcome of Procedure 1 with that of Procedure 3 shows that the time for children was more than four times greater, and more than twice as long for adults; this disproportionate increase is noteworthy. It will be recalled that the first situation allowed the subject to see all the numbers as he worked with them, while in the third he had to do them "in his head" after the experimenter had shown them briefly. By no stretch of imagination could this third task be considered complicated. Not for one moment could the instructions leave the subject in any doubt about the numbers concerned, and the numbers themselves are extremely small values. The experiment demonstrates how little "mental" arithmetic can be expected of children in the age group concerned, and apparently how little progress adults have made in this respect.

The addition time for Procedure 4 naturally invites comparison with Procedure 2. In both instances the numbers were presented in random order and had to be organized for the addition task. But in "2" the numbers were on the table, whereas in "4" the subject had to imagine the numbers being taken from the box in haphazard order. It might be conjectured that it would be easy to realize that putting the numbers into the box and taking them out again makes no essential change in the problem. Nevertheless the table shows that the time required for "4" increased sharply, being almost quadrupled for children and more than doubled for adults. The actual events in "4" are extremely simple, but apparently the experimenter's description of them has a confusing rather than an enlightening effect in this instance. The situation brings to mind Talleyrand's much-quoted paradox to the effect that words exist to hide meanings.

The results of the next three procedures—5, 6, and 7—are even more surprising.

The process of taking the numbers from the box in random order occurs once in Procedure 4, but is repeated twice in succession in Procedure 5. It would not seem particularly difficult to grasp the circumstances from the instructions and solve the problem easily by doubling the first sum arrived at, whether it is 15 for the children or 45 for the adults. The calculation requires only a small amount of time and should add little to the calculation time of "5" as compared with "4."

A separate study showed that the children took an average of 1.6 seconds to add 15 and 15 or multiply 2 times 15, and that the adults took approximately the same time to add 45 and 45 or multiply 2 times 45. Therefore, from the viewpoint of atomistic theory, the children would be expected to require an average addition time of 39.2 seconds in "5" and the adults should need 22.7 seconds. In reality the children's average rose to 67.7 seconds, or almost double the expected sum, and the adults' average is seen to have been 85.1 seconds, nearly four times what might have been expected. The differences are astonishingly large.

As an aid in evaluating Procedure 6, two auxiliary investigations were made: (a) Many children had difficulty in answering the question: "If I take one of the five numbers from the box, how big could it possibly be?" They were not accustomed to that type of problem. Nevertheless the difficulties were not extreme. When the question was put in isolation the answer required an average of 5.8 seconds. (b) It was also discovered that the time required to add 15 and 5 was, on the average, 1.5 seconds.

Regarded atomistically, calculation time for Procedure 6 should be greater than for Procedure 4. However, the time does not increase by 7.3 seconds (5.8 plus 1.5), but by 40.5 seconds, thus more than doubling the value in "4." In the case of adults the time for "6" might be expected to increase by 2.5 seconds, the time required to tell what the largest number would be, plus 2.7 seconds, the time required to add 45 and 9, or a total of 5.2 seconds. This would bring the adult time for "6" to 26.3 seconds. In reality the time taken was 56.3 seconds, more than double the theoretically anticipated result.

In the final experiment, Procedure 7, the task was to give the smallest, instead of the largest number that might be drawn from the box and added to the others. Considerations such as those already referred to would lead to the expectation that the calculation time for children would rise to 44.2 seconds. Actually it amounted to the extremely large figure of 113.4 seconds. A special study revealed that the concept "minimal" is more difficult for children than "maximal." This difference was not found in the case of adults, and for that reason their time for "7" was almost the same as for "6," being 54.2 seconds.

Proper interpretation of the experiments makes it particularly important to note the extensive agreement between the results for children and those for adults. Two facts should be emphasized. One is the increased difficulty that resulted from the wording of several comparatively simple procedures. Another, and even more significant finding, is the extreme degree to which the "doubling" problems became more difficult although each part could be solved quite simply by itself. Both of these circumstances cannot be dependent on the age factor. They must be attributed to general principles which apply to the thought process. They are inhibitions produced by the mutually unfavorable influence of segmental processes in the total process, which finds expression in marked retardation and increased numbers of errors. Such interference may be termed "connective inhibition" to distinguish it from other types of inhibition which have already been recognized.

A theory to explain connective inhibition will not be elaborated at this time. But its significance for thinking in everyday life should be emphasized, as well as the probability that it can be counteracted in the interest of efficient education in school and college.

Inhibition of simple thought processes is quite a different matter from a form of interference which was identified in the preceding chapter as "mental dazzle." Under its influence the psychophysical energy applied to thinking is disadvantageously distributed, with the result that the thought process consumes more time or is not completed.

As commonly used, the term "dazzle" refers to marked difficulty in visual perception, resulting from distinctly unfavorable illumination. It can occur when the illumination increases suddenly, to such an extent that the eyes cannot adapt themselves quickly enough to maintain perfect visual acuity. Dazzle can also be caused when the eyes are fully light adapted, if a considerable additional quantity of light wipes out the finer delineations of the retinal image. For instance, the details of a landscape are no longer easy to recognize when the observer faces into bright sunlight.

The two following illustrations were selected at random from a large number of cases of mental dazzle. In each one there are attendant circumstances which interfere with an examination of the structure of the problem, making the solution more difficult.

1. *The boat puzzle.* An officer and several soldiers come to a river. They cannot get to a bridge, but at the river bank there is a boat with two boys. The boat can carry two boys or one adult. How can the adults get across the river?

As is well known, the problem is solved in the following manner: The two boys row across the river. One gets out, and the other rows back. When he arrives he gets out and one adult rows across by himself. He, in turn, gets out and the boy on that bank travels back. In this manner the original situation is

restored and the whole procedure is repeated until all the adults
have been rowed to the opposite bank.

The number of adults, whether one, six, or more, is im-
material as far as the solution of the puzzle is concerned. In
view of the logical structure of the problem, the only critical
question is whether or not a method can be devised for rowing
one adult to the other bank. In the case of the second and third
it would merely be a matter of repeating the first process.
Nevertheless, experiments have shown that subjects do not regard the puzzle in that manner.

Two groups of students, 25 in each, were matched for tested
intelligence and were presented with the boat puzzle. The first
group was told that one adult was to be rowed across the river,
while the competing group was told there were six adults. The
former group solved the problem in an average time of 1½
minutes, while the latter group required approximately twice as
long. It is a fact, therefore, that raising the number of individuals to be transported increases the difficulty of the puzzle
to a marked degree. It has the effect of obscuring the structure
of the task and its execution.

It is more laborious to row six adults than to row one, and
it would appear that this thought plays a part in the outcome of
the experiment. The larger number has a confusing influence,
reduces "mental energy" at a critical moment, and retards the
thought process. The attendant circumstance, "six adults,"
produces mental dazzle.

Visual dazzle increases with the brilliance of the light, but it
cannot simply be assumed that the disturbing attendant circumstances in *thinking* are in direct proportion to their effect. It
makes little difference in the subject's calculation speed, whether
there are 6, 10, or 12 adults in the puzzle. In fact it is probable that when the number is increased radically, possibly to
1000, the problem acquires a humorous tone and assists the
subject in realizing that it need be solved only for "one."

2. *The "Rule of Three."* A procedure for solving many problems, among them the calculation of interest, is termed the "rule
of three," and is often practiced thoroughly in schools.

The specific problem concerned is this:

How much interest does a capital of $800 earn in 2 years if the rate is 4 per cent?

The details of the problem are arranged for solution in this formula:

$$X = \frac{4 \cdot 800 \cdot 2}{100}$$

Various matched groups of students have been timed while arriving at the formula under varying conditions. For some students the figures for capital, rate of interest, and number of years were comparatively simple, while for others they were replaced by more involved data.

It should be emphasized that the assignment was not to carry out the calculation, but only to set up the proper formula for solving the problem.

Results show that the time consumed in setting up the formula increases considerably when the capital is changed from $800 to $875 or $875.36, the interest rate is changed from 4 per cent to 3.5 per cent or 3.75 per cent, and the number of years, instead of 2, becomes 23 or 23½. The more complex the numbers seem to the students, the stronger the mental dazzle becomes. Apparently realization that actual calculation, if required, would be troublesome, interferes with solution of a part of the problem with which anticipated difficulty of that sort has no logical connection whatsoever. As indicated, the students had been informed specifically that they would be required merely to set up the formula, but not complete the calculations.

Piaget defines logic as the axiomatics of reason, and states that the corresponding experimental science is psychology. He adds: "An axiomatic system cannot fill the place of its corresponding inductive science for the simple but fundamental reason that its own purity is nothing more than a never-attainable terminal state" (1948, page 44).

Mental dazzle appears particularly we.. suited to emphasize the contrast between logic, which deals with the formal connections between the objects of thinking, and the defective manner in which those objects actually are comprehended subjectively.

CHAPTER 23

THE TRANSPOSITION OF ACTION FORMS

Ehrenfels' observations on the transposition of tunes were undoubtedly among Gestalt psychology's most decisive arguments against the atomistic viewpoint in psychology. It was Ehrenfels who pointed out that a tune remains the same even if it is so displaced in the scale that every single note is changed.

At times the transposition of tunes is discussed as if the essence of a tune were a mere sequence of notes. After all, proponents of this view suggest, it is the sequence of notes which is transposed. However, it should be observed that the organization of the notes with respect to timing, or rhythm, approaches their sequence in importance as far as a particular tune experience is concerned. Even if the sequence of notes is retained a tune cannot be recognized if the rhythm is altered beyond a certain point. Playful syncopation of classical music can be carried only that far if the original music is to be identifiable. If rhythmic structure were unimportant it would be impossible to recognize a tune when it is tapped out with a pencil.

The writer conducted an experiment to determine the extent to which tapped rhythm could produce tune recognition. The project involved 56 subjects. The task was to recognize the tapped rhythms of the five familiar Swedish tunes, among which was the Swedish national anthem. Results were as follows:

On the average, 2.85 of the five tunes were recognized. All of the tunes were recognized by 5 participants, and four were correctly named by 14. The tune most commonly identified was the national anthem, with 44 recognitions. Only one subject scored no recognition at all; as he himself stated, he appeared to have "no ear for music."

There is a fertile field for further study of rhythm as a determining factor in tunes. It can already be stated, however, that rhythm alone can definitely produce recognition of a familiar tune. In reality, then, at least one factor, rhythm, does remain identical when a tune is transposed. This fact does not invalidate other investigations of tune transposition. But a study of the significance of rhythm as a separate factor in tune creation would have clarified the situation.

A question that naturally arises is the range of rhythm variation within which tune recognition is possible. Even without a searching investigation it may be presumed that the range is wide. No musician always plays a piece in exactly the same measure. A record can be played at greatly varying speeds without significantly altering the nature of the music.

Depending on their temperaments, different conductors interpret the same music with different timing. The terms *presto* and *largo* express only relative differences, and are not absolute standards. As determined by a Mälzel metronome they may vary as follows, in terms of beats per minute:

> *Presto:* 208–188
> *Allegro:* 188–150
> *Andante:* 150–125
> *Adagio:* 125–98
> *Larghetto:* 98–71
> *Largo:* 71–41

The value of the quarter note is taken to be 60/96, or about ⅔ second.

Another conclusion which requires no experimental confirmation is that there are rhythm speeds below which and above which rhythm cannot serve to identify a tune. The tune disintegrates when it is played too slowly, because it cannot be comprehended as a unit. When it is played too quickly the listener is unable to analyze it.

Perception of music is primarily concerned with sensory forms. However, this raises a question about motor, or action forms. Can they, too, be transposed? Again everyday experiences favor an affirmative reply. A waltz can be danced more rapidly at one time than another. A horse can walk slowly or quickly. But his quick walk need not cause him to make more rapid progress than a slow trot. A fast trot, in turn, can result in less speed than a slow gallop. Thus the horse can make use of three distinct methods of locomotion, and each is transposable.

A study of the psychology of sports was conducted by the writer, to indicate the manner in which a runner alters his speed in a race. In spite of the amazing regularity of his total pattern of movements he can easily change the speed with which he executes that pattern. After a side glance at his competitors he steps up his pace; later he may slow down again.

It was a physiologist, von Kries, who called attention to the particular aspect of transposition under consideration. He stated:

One can voluntarily determine the tempo of certain practiced movements in advance, and within wide limits. Apparently such variation affects the total process only as far as speed is concerned. One can play the very same piece of music slowly or quickly, either by choice or instruction. I recall from my military experience that the gun drill was carried out much more slowly in a company than in either a regiment or a brigade. Since a drill sounds most orderly when all concerned seize the rifle grip with as much coordination as possible, this difference naturally caused some difficulty. Nevertheless it was not greatly disturbing. It was easy to see that in spite of long, thorough practice at one speed it was possible to shift immediately to another.

Tranposition of action forms can be considered a fact. But the details of its operation remain a question. Two varieties of experimentation were carried out to supply an answer.* The first to be described was concerned with transposition of "abstract," relatively complex series of beats, while the second dealt with a common skill, writing.

1. Equipment for the rhythm investigation consisted of a Morse telegraph apparatus rebuilt to permit graphic recording of rhythmic tapping.

The usual procedure was to have the experimenter tap out a rhythm which the subject was then instructed to repeat on the

---

* Conducted by T. Künnapas under the direction of the writer.

telegraph apparatus. Righthanded and lefthanded subjects were permitted to use the preferred hand. Perfect reproduction of the experimenter's rhythm was not required, since the purpose of the experiment was to determine the precision with which the subject could transpose a rhythm he himself had tapped out, rather than the "model" with which he began.

After the subject had tapped out a rhythm in the manner described he was instructed to repeat it, first more quickly, then more slowly. He was not told how much he should increase or decrease the tempo. In each case he repeated the rhythm fifteen times in succession. This procedure made it possible to establish the duration of the first reproduction, the average time values of the transposed forms, and their variability.

The subjects seemed to regard their experimental task as a natural one. They behaved as if they were accustomed to such activity. Yet it may be assumed that they had never before carried out a truly similar assignment in transposition. This fact is interesting in connection with the striking success with which the rhythms were transposed. Neither previous practice nor brief practice in anticipation of the task can account for it.

The first results to be described were obtained with a three-beat rhythm in this form:

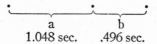

As shown, interval "a" was 1.048 seconds and interval "b" was .496 second. The ratio between "a" and "b" may be designated as quotient "Q," and amounts in this instance to 2.133. Similarly obtained quotients for faster and slower reproduction may then be represented by the symbols "Q_f" and "Q_s" respectively.

Results in the case of an unusually skillful subject showed that the difference between "Q" and "Q_f" was only 1.6 per cent. The difference between "Q" and "Q_s" was no more than 2.3 per cent. It is evident that motor transposition of the sort concerned in the experiment can be carried out with great precision.

The average results for twelve subjects show less precision than the single instance described. The difference between "Q"

and "Q_f" was 6.8 per cent, while "Q" and "Q_s" differed by 8.4 per cent. The average difference was 7.6 per cent. Similar results were obtained with transposition of other rhythms.

The outcome seems paradoxical if it is not studied from the viewpoint of Gestalt psychology. The matter was clarified by further experiments in which a simple rhythm was made part of a more extensive and more complex rhythm. The simple rhythm pictured in the diagram above was made into a complex rhythm in which the simple form was repeated several times:

. ...　...　.. .

It is interesting to note that the average differences for the complex form were 6 per cent for faster reproduction and 6.1 per cent for slower reproduction. This is considerably less than the 7.6 per cent obtained for the simple rhythm alone.

In a later procedure an even more complicated rhythm was employed. Again it included repetitions of the simple rhythm:

... .

Transposition of this last rhythm produced differences which were still smaller. They were 4.8 per cent for faster reproduction and 5.4 per cent for slower reproduction.

What is the significance of these findings? They demonstrate that it is easier to transpose a simple rhythm when it is part of a longer, more complex rhythm than when it is by itself. The outcome is another apparently paradoxical conclusion which can be explained by a Gestalt principle. The whole fixes its parts more securely and adds to their distinguishing characteristics, producing greater pregnance and making transposition easier. It is reasonable to anticipate an upper limit for this phenomenon, and that increasing complexity of rhythm would finally invalidate the tendency described.

It would be of considerable interest to determine whether or not the principle evolved for transposition of rhythms also applies to transposition of note sequences, or perhaps the transposition of visual forms. Could it be proved that in those cases, too, a part can be transposed more successfully when it is set in a more complex whole? An affirmative result seems probable.

Attention has been called to the fact that there are limits to the increase and decrease in speed which will permit transposition of rhythms. Experiments were devised to set these limits precisely.

Again the rhythm form . . . was employed, and the scheme for designating its time values was the same as that already described. The subject was required to beat out this rhythm more and more rapidly. Subsequently he was instructed to repeat it more and more slowly. Table 3 indicates the size of "a," "b," quotient "Q," and the per cent of difference from the initial quotient "Q." Six series are shown for acceleration and six series for deceleration, in terms of averages for fifteen subjects whose performance was highly consistent.

The beginning values of "a" and "b" are not equal for acceleration and deceleration because, as was stated, the procedure did not require the subjects to imitate the experimenter's model rhythm exactly.

Repetition of the experiment with slight variations in the values of "a" and "b" produced similar results.

TABLE 6

VARIABILITY OF RHYTHM REPRODUCTION WITH ACCELERATED AND DECELERATED PERFORMANCE

Series	Acceleration (in thousandths of a second)				Deceleration (in thousandths of a second)			
	a	b	Q	Per Cent of Deviation from Base Quotient	a	b	Q	Per Cent of Deviation from Base Quotient
1	.679	.351	1.938	....	.387	.224	1.724	....
2	.548	.282	1.947	5	.527	.295	1.788	3.7
3	.464	.240	1.930	4	.629	.363	1.733	5
4	.268	.139	1.930	4	1.289	.771	1.670	3.1
5	.232	.120	1.924	7	1.876	1.492	1.264	26.7
6	.122	.108	1.128	41.8	2.319	2.196	1.056	38.7

Findings may be summarized as follows:

Transposition of a rhythm of approximately one second in duration can be carried out with great precision within wide limits. For accelerated as well as decelerated reproduction these limits are in a ratio of about 1 to 3, or a total ratio of 1 to 6 for both directional changes in speed taken together.

It is only natural to ask why transposition fails beyond the limits mentioned. In the case of the shortest intervals, as shown in Series 6 of Table 6, the values of "a" and "b" were .122 and .108 respectively. In that series the per cent of deviation increased from 7 per cent to 41.82 per cent. There the subject arrived at the point where he was making the most rapid movements of which he was capable. Good control was no longer in his power.

For deceleration, it can be seen in Series 5 of Table 3 that the combined time of "a" and "b" was 3.368 seconds. The precision at that point sank from a variation of 3.1 per cent in Series 4 to 26.7 per cent in Series 5. There the time span exceeded William Stern's "psychological present." Only within that span is direct perception of time possible.

It has been emphasized that subjects do not regard the task of transposing a tapped rhythm as unusual. Yet the task is unusual, and the findings cannot be attributed to practice. That is not to say that transposition cannot be improved with practice. On the contrary, experiments designed to settle that question have shown that such improvement does take place. It can be assumed that this also holds true for transposition of tunes.

If the same rhythm is tapped out as often as 15 times in succession with the same intervals, the relationship between the rhythm and the intervals which separate its parts assumes special characteristics. The relationship between the rhythms as acoustic forms and the intervals as acoustic backgrounds is similar to the relationship between visual forms and their backgrounds. No matter how little the visual background is noticed, and no matter how low its conscious attention value may be, there would be no form without that background. By analogy, no matter how little the intervals between the acoustic forms are noticed, and no matter how low their conscious attention value may be, without them there would be no rhythms set off in relief.

Time intervals have so little attention value that the impression they make might be termed "nothingness." Yet it is hardly surprising that they have a marked effect on rhythm, and that rhythm in turn exerts considerable influence on the intervals. It has been shown that when the subject concentrates exclusively on the rhythm, he maintains the intervals themselves with astonishing consistency. Their variability, when repeated by the subject, is only slightly greater than that of the rhythms, which are the focus of attention. If the subject is told to increase or decrease the speed of the rhythms, the intervals involved are decreased or increased in almost direct proportion although no instructions whatsoever are given with respect to them.

Rhythm forms and their time interval backgrounds are so closely interrelated that a change in reproduction of the intervals causes a change in reproduction of the rhythm forms. The following experiments demonstrate this fact:

Subjects were asked to tap out fifteen successive double beats. The diagram represents the double beats with the letters "a," "b," and "c." Intervals are shown as "x," "y," etc.

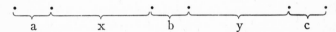

The double beats were timed at .428 second, but the length of the intervals between double beats was not prescribed. As an example it may be reported that one subject chose intervals of 1.311 seconds for "x," "y," etc.

As a measure of precision for the timing of the double beats their fifteen single values were averaged and divided by their average deviation. The resulting quotient for precision of the double beats was 1/31. By a similar process a quotient for precision of the intervals between the double beats was calculated as 1/33. Remarkably enough, with respect to these samplings, the intervals with their small attention value varied less than the rhythm forms, which were in the center of consciousness.

The subject was then asked to repeat the double beat for a second series of fifteen successive trials. But this time he was instructed to make the intervals irregular. As a result the precision quotient for the rhythm form was reduced to 1/11. This was about a third of the measure obtained for the rhythm forms when there were no instructions about the intervals. It will be recalled that they had actually turned out to be extremely consistent. The subject reported that it was decidedly difficult to tap out the double beats as a separate problem rather than to regard them as a unit together with the intervals.

The principles governing the relationship between acoustic forms and their backgrounds open a new field for research. The brief study reported shows its possibilities.

2. The second series of experiments was designed to ascertain the reliability with which action forms can be transposed. The act of writing was selected because it lends itself to comparatively simple experimental techniques.

The scriptochronograph * was used to investigate the Gestalt principles of writing. It records the time element in handwriting with any desired degree of accuracy. It has the additional advantage of registering time directly from the act of writing itself, making additional apparatus, such as a stop watch, unnecessary.

The scriptochronograph makes use of a chemically prepared paper on which script is produced by an electrochemical process. The writing instrument is a metal stylus, serving as a positive pole, to which current is conducted by a thin, highly flexible wire. The writing paper is dipped for a short time in a colorless solution of potassium thyocyanate and is then allowed to dry until only a trace of moisture remains. The paper rests on an aluminum plate which acts as a conductor, and forms the "desk." With steadily flowing current, use of the stylus produces a distinct, dark brown script, the dark brown color being a precipitate of ferric thiocyanate.

Three details should be added. A wood frame keeps the paper pressed firmly against the metal plate. It was found preferable to have the plate slightly concave because that shape caused the paper to adhere more closely to it. The optimal dampness of the paper depends on its thickness and consistency.

---

* Designed by the writer (1948). Information, C. S. Stoelting and Co., Chicago, Ill.

When the scriptochronograph is in actual use to measure the time factors in handwriting, a continuous flow of current is not applied to the stylus. Instead, the current is interrupted a specific number of times during a given period. As a result, the script does not consist of continuous lines, but forms a series of dots or dashes with intervening spaces. This occurs when the duration of the closed circuit, producing a brown dot, is short compared with the duration of the open circuit, which leaves the spaces between the dots.

If there are thirty interruptions of current per second the space between each two dots represents 1/30 second. If under these conditions a single letter consists of fifteen dot-space units it means that the subject took ½ second to write it. The size of the spaces between dots naturally varies with the speed of the writing; however, in general the measurement of time is accurate to 1/100 second.

The experiments to be described were carried out with thirty electric impulses per second, a rate well adapted to adult subjects accustomed to writing. Fewer impulses per second must be employed for children who write slowly, or for adults who do not write with ease.

It might be suspected that interpretation of script would be difficult when a dot happens to be exactly at the crossing of two lines. However, in practice it is invariably possible to assign the dot to its proper line by noting its position with reference to the dots which precede and follow the point of intersection. If two dots happen to be at precisely the same place, the fact is almost always obvious because the double dot is more heavily marked.

A more serious drawback might have been encountered in timing such letters as "t," "m," and "n," because they require the pen to travel the same path more than once. Fortunately experience with electrolytic writing has shown that retracing appears clearly in practically every instance and can be analyzed for its time value. In fact the scriptochronograph proves serviceable under just those circumstances which would render other methods useless.

The wire attached to the stylus raises an understandable question. Does it interfere with the natural quality of hand movements in writing? In practical use the wire is hardly noticeable. No subjects reported it as disturbing. Such reassurance is helpful, but insufficient proof, and a special study was made of the problem. Subjects produced two samples of handwriting, one with an ordinary pen and the other with the electric stylus. There was no recognizable difference between them.

Other investigators making use of apparatus to study writing have not regarded the changed writing situation as a serious source of error. One example was the research conducted with Kraepelin's writing scale. Another was Pedersen's study, in the course of which he made use of a penholder which measured finger pressure by means of a pneumatic device.

The scriptochronograph was used in two experiments designed to trace the transposition of handwriting movements:

1. To what extent is the rhythm of handwriting maintained when its size is varied? The first experiment sought an answer to this question.

Each subject was instructed to write script of varying size. He was to begin writing script of a size usual for him, and then to write in larger and larger script in four successive steps. No directions were given as to the details of this process. They were left to the individual subject. The word to be written was "elev."

The outcome of the study may be seen in Table 7. Figures are in terms of averages for one subject whose performance was representative of the group averages.

The largest sample of handwriting was approximately five times larger than the normal sample, a considerable difference. Somewhat similar results were obtained with respect to the size of individual letters. The first "e" increased by about 5.5, the "l" by 4.1, the second "e" by 5.6, and the "v" by 5.1. Only the "l" failed to follow the trend as decidedly as did the other letters, but the variation was slight. Perfect consistency was not to be expected.

The time values remained remarkably constant throughout the changes in size, for individual letters as well as the total word. Time for the first "e," the "l," and the "v" were iden-

TABLE 7

TIME REQUIRED BY A REPRESENTATIVE SUBJECT TO WRITE "ELEV" IN
HANDWRITING OF INCREASING SIZE

Trials	"e"		"l"		"e"		"v"		Total Time in Seconds for Whole Word
	Length in mm	Time in Seconds	Length in mm.	Time in Seconds	Length in mm.	Time in Seconds	Length in mm.	Time in Seconds	
1. Normal	7.4	.23	13.2	.30	7.	.22	7.5	.22	.97
2. Enlarged I	13.1	.23	20.5	.30	12.5	.21	11.4	.22	.96
3. Enlarged II	20.7	.24	31.2	.31	18.3	.21	20.3	.24	.98
4. Enlarged III	26.	.23	44.8	.29	26.8	.23	26.	.24	.99
5. Enlarged IV	40.7	.26	53.6	.30	39.	.23	38.9	.24	1.03
Average time in seconds for each letter and whole word		.24		.30		.22		.23	.99

tical in three different trials, while the deviations in other instances were very small. Time values for the word as a whole differ from each other by only a few hundredths of a second. How may the outcome be explained?

Apparently speed of writing adjusts itself to size of writing with surprising precision; speed increases in direct proportion to size. Rhythm of movement is maintained and transposed almost perfectly. These statements hold true, in any event, for the conditions of the experiment described.

Recalling that there were limits to transposition of abstract rhythms, it is equally logical to expect limits for transposition of handwriting as speed decreases or increases. These limits remain to be determined.

2. The second experiment was designed to discover the effect of increased speed on handwriting movement.

Again the subject was required to write the word "elev" under four varying conditions. But this time he was to begin by writing at normal speed and increase the rate at the second trial. In the third trial he was to write as fast as possible. Finally he was to write very slowly.

Table 8 presents the values obtained by a subject whose record represents the average of other participants.

TABLE 8

APPORTIONMENT OF TOTAL WRITING TIME TO LETTERS OF THE WORD
"ELEV" WRITTEN AT VARYING SPEEDS
(In terms of seconds)

Trials	"e"	"l"	"e"	"v"
1. NORMAL. Total time 1.42	.37	.32	.30	.43
Per cent of total time	26.	22.5	21.	30.
2. ACCELERATED. Total time 1.09	.29	.26	.23	.31
Per cent of total time	26.2	24.2	20.8	28.8
Per cent of deviation from Trial 1	.8	7.5	1.	5.6
				Average deviation from Trial 1: 3.7
3. MAXIMAL ACCELERATION. Total time .89	.23	.21	.19	.26
Per cent of total time	26.	23.6	21.	29.4
Per cent of deviation from Trial 1	0.	4.9	0.	3.6
				Average deviation from Trial 1: 2.1
4. DECELERATED. Total time 2.06	.5	.48	.44	.64
Per cent of total time	24.2	23.2	21.2	31.2
Per cent of deviation from Trial 1	5.2	3.1	1.	2.3
				Average deviation from Trial 1: 2.9

Table 8 shows that the time required to write the word at normal speed is 1.42 seconds, and increases to .89 second at maximal acceleration. This change of approximately 55 per cent is less than might be expected by observing a subject or doing the writing oneself.

The instruction to write slowly produces a speed of 2.06 seconds for the total word. This is .65 second greater than normal speed as seen in Trial 1, and is an acceleration of almost 40 per cent. Subjectively the impression of increased speed is considerably higher.

The table also shows the effect of acceleration and deceleration on the per cent of total time devoted to each individual letter. Average deviations from normal speed are seen to be

3.7 per cent for acceleration in Trial 2, 2.1 per cent for Trial 3; for deceleration in Trial 4 the figure is 2.9 per cent.

The conclusion is that the rhythmic movements of hand-writing remain essentially constant in a wide range of speed variations.

CHAPTER 24

VOLITION AND EMOTION IN EDUCATION

At one time discussion of voluntary action was genetically oriented. Reflexes were described as its innate basis, and mature voluntary behavior was said to come about through facilitation and inhibition. This approach made it easy to overlook the dynamic nature of volition. A system of reflexes leaves no room for spontaneity nurtured by internal forces.

Gestalt psychologists were not the first to recognize the necessity for seeking the propellants of behavior, any more than they were the first to point out that such forces appear as needs, drives, and instincts. But the Gestalt theorists who dealt with volition took up the problem and dealt with it in a characteristic manner. The result is a contribution to their theory of the dynamics of behavior.

The Gestalt view of the dynamics of perception must be supplemented if it is to explain internally aroused behavior. The perceptual field structures itself even when the subject's attitude is passive. Stimuli, of and by themselves, never determine behavior. Behavior is determined by inner tensions, based on needs. These tensions decide how the subject will respond to various stimuli. The same perceptual field structures itself in one way for a hungry individual, and in quite another way for one who is satiated. The landscape is organized differently for a soldier seeking cover, as opposed to an artist looking for a scene to paint. It may delight a misanthrope to be the only person in a house, but depress a sociably inclined individual.

A need establishes the value of an object for a particular kind of behavior. A letter box is a positive incentive only when it is needed. A bench is inviting only if one tires of walking. The neutral object becomes one capable of influencing behavior only under the pressure of a need.

The relationship between internal processes and manifest effect is particularly clear in the psychology of needs. When a need arises, imagery focuses on the means of satisfying it and impels the individual toward it unless an external barrier interferes.

Everyone knows the agitated movement of an animal in the zoo when feeding time approaches. Hunger acts as a vector driving it toward the food. It paces back and forth, pressing against the barrier of the bars to get as close as possible to the goal.

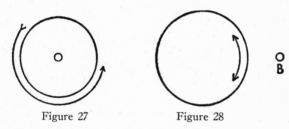

Figure 27   Figure 28

Figure 27 represents a circular fence with food in the center. The arrow shows the path of a dog or chicken whose hunger vector drives it around the fence for a considerable length of time. Figure 28 varies the situation by having a ball, "B," outside a circular playpen. In this instance the arrow represents the path of a child walking back and forth at the part of the pen nearest the ball. If the playpen has an opening on the opposite side the child may take the roundabout path made necessary by the barrier, go through the opening and then to the goal. Such behavior is possible only if the child is sufficiently mature to survey the total situation and first move away from the goal as a preliminary to approaching it later.

It was Lewin (1936) who studied behavior like that of the child in the playpen and developed the concept of topological, or vector psychology. The self is viewed as a part of the topological structure of the behavioral field. The objects which constitute the field influence the self, whose needs, in turn, play a part in determining the nature of the field.

If an important task is being performed by an individual, but is interrupted by some new duty, both tension systems can exist side by side as separate entities. According to Lewin a mixture of the two acts, such as the "contamination" in slips of the tongue, seldom occurs. The researcher preoccupied with a scientific problem can stop to do justice to a hearty meal; the meal itself may be interrupted by a telephone call. The various tension systems exist undisturbed next to each other in the individual. The self coordinates them by volition.

Lewin states (page 168) : "Between summative togetherness and the completely unified whole of a strong Gestalt, in which parts completely lose their independence, there exists a continuous transition (dynamically weak forms)."

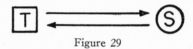

Figure 29

Figure 29 shows that subject "S" is simultaneously attracted and repelled by a difficult task, "T." He is in a conflict situation. There is an equilibrium, but it involves considerable tension

Lewin regarded an act such as a decision to take a walk as the setting up of a "quasi need." Topological psychology considers an individual already engaged in planned behavior as in an intermediate stage as far as vectors are concerned. Activity indicates unreleased tension. Habits and technical skills are not sources of mental energy, but are simply employed in the service of needs, somewhat like tools.

It will be recalled that an experiment demonstrated the greater memory value of unfinished as opposed to completed tasks. Vector psychology supplies an explanation for this finding. It may be attributed to the tension which arises when an undertaking sets up a "quasi need."

Unreleased tension also accounts for the tendency to return to interrupted tasks. Or, if it is impossible to resume the same activity, another may serve as a substitute. It is as if a person were unable to obtain the food he really prefers, and satisfies his hunger with something he likes less. Finally, if no substitution is possible, he may retire into unreality and continue his activity in phantasy. A person who is hungry but has nothing to eat allows his phantasy free play in imaginary satisfaction.

When a subject is compelled to carry out a monotonous task, such as writing the same letter again and again over a long period of time, the result is mental satiation which makes it completely impossible to continue. If still more pressure is put on the subject he may get a writer's cramp which will emphasize his inability to comply. It is easy to see the significance of these findings for an understanding of certain forms of psychopathology. The inability to continue writing is not due to general fatigue. A clear distinction must be made between fatigue and satiation. The hand which is unable to continue writing monotonous rows of letters can function immediately if the assignment is changed to drawing geometric figures.

Topological vector psychology is well adapted to studying and clarifying many problems of volition. Nevertheless, by placing so much emphasis on the field it leaves no suitable place for spontaneity of the self, which can set goals of its own accord.

Lewin applied the topological viewpoint to educational problems. He believed teaching would achieve better and more lasting results if personal participation in activities could be substituted for reward and punishment, which are so often unrelated to the subject matter. To enable a child to participate, his activity must be made part of another more inclusive activity in which he engages gladly and spontaneously. If one activity is imbedded in another in this manner, its meaning is changed, and as a result the child's attitude toward it is altered.

Lewin stated that: "A child that does not like a certain food eats it without more ado if the goblin on the end of the spoon is to be buried, or if the spoon, as a train, is to enter the station of the mouth" (1936, page 168).

Cod liver oil, with its repulsive taste, is taken more easily if it seems necessary in a game of "doctor and patient." In these examples the original activity—eating or taking medicine—becomes a dependent part of the more inclusive total activity.

When a school assignment can be imbedded in some activity with a practical purpose it often loses its odious qualities. Some children readily do arithmetic problems when they are made part of "playing store," although they would not want to do them just "for school."

It is always important to make sure that imbedding produces genuinely strong activity forms, which will not easily disintegrate. Modern primers for the first reading lessons have been embellished with pictures to make the dry material more appealing. This undoubtedly represents progress by comparison with the unrelieved dull appearance of earlier primers. But from a psychological point of view the pictures are loosely connected with the reading assignment.

The Decroly global method of teaching reading is preferable because it does not begin with single letters, but with short words or even brief sentences. These allow the child to read meaningful communications very quickly and later to write them out. The Decroly method makes use of the principle of imbedding.

Children find it particularly difficult to take up an isolated activity because of the greater dynamic unity which characterizes their age. The meaningful whole in which the child's separate acts are imbedded should be chosen with special care.

The principle of psychological imbedding is by no means applicable solely to children. It is only necessary to note how often—in the international sphere of diplomacy or in the "diplomacy" of everyday life—success may depend on imbedding an unpleasant request in a larger, more agreeable piece of business.

To date Gestalt psychology has devoted remarkably little attention to emotion. This cannot be accounted for merely on the basis of the subjective nature of emotions, which do not seem to lend themselves so readily to Gestalt methods. Koffka (1935, pages 325–327) himself called attention to facts which opposed earlier assumptions that all emotions are related to the self. A landscape may appear cheerful, mountains may seem majestic, and the stirred-up sea can have a threatening aspect, but in such instances it cannot be said that emotions are transferred from the self in accordance with Lipps's theory of empathy.

It is most probable that the comparatively unstructured nature of emotions has held little attraction for Gestalt research. Stern (1935) was emphatic in stating that emotions are the least organized phenomena because they are the ones most deeply imbedded in the individual. Krueger (1920) was of the same opinion. The most searching study was made by Lewin in connection with his investigations of volitional psychology. These dealt with the dynamics of emotion, or, more specifically, of affect.

CHAPTER 25

MEDICAL PSYCHOLOGY

Gestalt theory has had a marked influence on medical psychology. Goldstein's and Gelb's investigations of individuals with brain injury deserve particular attention.

Partial destruction of the optic nerves or the visual brain cortex may cause hemianopsia. An individual with this condition can see only half of the visual field. In a clear-cut hemianopsia a vertical line divides the visual field almost exactly in half; depending on the location of his injury the subject may be unable to see what is to the left or to the right of the dividing line. The half which remains functional undergoes a characteristic reorganization which Gestalt theory makes comprehensible.

Hemianopsia is often betrayed by mistakes which the injured individual makes in dealing with objects. He may reach past them, either too far to the left or too far to the right, the direction being determined by the site of his lesion. If he is told to look the examiner straight in the eye, it can be observed that he does not fixate directly, but seems to look somewhat to one side. The deviation is small, but there is an astonishingly acute appreciation of whether or not the other person is looking directly into one's eyes.

Why does the hemianoptic individual have difficulty in fixating properly? Why does he not focus so that the object's reflected rays fall directly on the center of the retina? It is because the defective visual field has been reorganized. It has been reorganized in such a way that it forms the optimal total visual field. As a result, the impression of "straight ahead" no longer extends from the *fovea centralis,* but from a location to one side of it. A new center has been developed in the half of the retina which continues to function, and that particular location has acquired better visual acuity than it possessed previously.

The new center of vision does not remain automatically fixed, like the old one. It has only a functional existence, and changes its location with the task faced by the subject. If, for instance, he reads words of various length, the new *fovea centralis* lies further toward the functioning side in the case of longer words, and less in that direction in the case of shorter words.

The altered functioning described is reminiscent of an animal's reorganized motor functioning when it has lost one or more limbs. In a similar way the sensory field is reorganized when half of it has been destroyed. Both reorganizations take place in such a manner that remaining functions can continue to meet external demands as well as possible under the circumstances. The older theory of localization is utterly incapable of explaining such readjustment.

The following techniques serve to illustrate the Gestalt interpretation of hemianopsia:

The hemianoptic subject is shown a circle. It is exposed for too brief a time to permit any eye movements. The circle is placed in such a position that only half its image falls on the functioning half of the retina, while the other half falls on the blind half. If the subject is asked to state what he sees, he reports that he sees a complete circle, not merely a semicircle.

In a variation of the procedure the patient is again shown a circle, but it is arranged to have more than half its image fall on the defective half of the retina. This time he does not report seeing a full circle, but only an arc. Apparently the defective half cannot assist in completing the visual figure under these conditions.

As a third version of the experiment an ellipse is shown to the subject so that half of it falls on the functioning portion of the retina, and the other half on the defective side. He reports that he sees only half the ellipse. But if he is shown a larger part of the ellipse he reports seeing all of it.

The results seem contradictory. But Goldstein and Gelb attribute them to the pregnance tendency of figures viewed by hemianoptic subjects. Here the concept of endogenous form pressure finds interesting confirmation and supplementation. If one part of a whole is so constituted that it "decrees" the nature of the whole, the gap can be filled in by the nonfunctioning area of the visual field. That occurred in the case of the half circle, which the subject saw as a full circle. When less than a half circle was shown the continuation of its outline was not "decreed," but was left an open question, and recognition of a full circle was impossible. Half of an ellipse does not fully reveal the nature of the whole figure of which it is a part. It could be a part of several sorts of curves. The whole ellipse is completed by the subject only when he is shown more than half of it because its total nature is then revealed, or "decreed." A hemianoptic individual sees a whole figure when its visible portion—that portion whose image falls on the functioning area of the retina—is sufficient to determine the nature of the whole figure.

Two other pertinent questions require an answer:

What occurs when the patient is shown a straight line, only half of which lies in the functioning half of the visual field? Does he see the whole line or only half of it? He sees only half the line, because the determination of a straight line depends on its straightness, rather than its absolute length.

What does the subject report when he is shown half of a symmetrical letter, such as an "A"? Does he recognize the whole letter? He does not, because "A" is not formed in such a way that half of it determines the total letter. Gestalt psychology can make good use of this fact in refuting the older view that individual experience plays a decisive role in recognition of figures. If that view were correct, the letter "A," which has been experienced any number of times, should be easy to recognize when only a portion of it is shown. Both the total letter and its constituent parts should be thoroughly familiar.

CHAPTER 26

COMPARATIVE PSYCHOLOGY

In an earlier chapter it was suggested that the Gestalt approach would be particularly applicable wherever mental processes occur in a naïve, natural manner, little influenced by deliberation. Genetic psychology appears to fill these requirements admirably, and the expectation proves to be justified. A chapter will be devoted to each of the three major branches of genetic psychology, which are the comparative, child, and social areas. The first-named is the subject of the present chapter.

Purely instinctive behavior occurs only in animals. Predominance of instinct means rigidity in carrying out the most vital life functions. But it is not only the animal's instinctual behavior which reveals greater rigidity. The animal is also in the grip of holistic processes in other respects. For instance, color form responses which were not at all explainable on an atomistic basis were first demonstrated in animals.

Movement forms are of great importance for certain animals. They are completely unresponsive to an animal which ordinarily serves as their food, if the prey is motionless or moves in an unusual manner. Dragonflies live on gnats which they pursue in flight. But they die of hunger before attacking gnats which crawl on the wall. A cuttlefish tries to seize crabs only if they are swimming, but pays no attention to them if they crawl on the sea bottom. It reacts only to the crab's characteristic swimming pattern. The crab is not recognized if it moves differently.

The reaction of animals to objects is influenced more by their position in the total field than is the case with humans. Bees have difficulty in finding the entrance to their hive if it is shifted a little toward the back or to one side. They continue to fly to the previous location of the entrance. Apparently bees do not experience the hive as an object by itself; instead it seems to be a part of its surroundings, nearby or further distant, and the total situation determines their behavior toward the hive entrance.

Another pertinent illustration is supplied by the heron. The young of this bird greet the returning male parent after specific ceremonial behavior on his part. But if under unusual circumstances he omits this greeting, the young birds assume a threatening attitude toward him and peck at his head. Their treatment of him is inconsistent, varying with the form of the total situation.

Objects dealt with by animals become imbedded in unitary behavior forms with strong emotional tone, and variations evoke entirely different responses. Man, too, reacts to perceptual forms. But what primarily distinguishes him from animals is that he can emancipate himself. No perceptual form is so strong that a human being cannot break it up. The very fact that he can assume an atomistic attitude is the most convincing proof of the extent to which man can liberate himself from the compulsion of natural forms.

Even memory forms bind animals more tightly than humans. An animal is far more subject to the force of habit. If it has once learned to take an indirect route it often continues to take it even if the barrier which made the route necessary is removed. Unless he is absent-minded a human being can free himself from an accustomed mode of behavior.

Koffka (1935, pages 403–406) defines an instinct as an innate capacity for gaps and their closure. This formulation is so general that it includes considerably more than instinct. Some Gestalt psychologists believe that the instinct concept no longer requires the assumption of goal striving or a specific tendency toward self-preservation. They substitute the principle of organic self-regulation and maintenance of present status. Gestalt psychology believes firmly in the meaningfulness of instinctive behavior.

The closed quality of instinctive behavior has often led to analogy with a tune. Just as a tune acquires meaning only after its single notes have been combined, instinctive behavior becomes meaningful only when its phases have been combined to form a whole unit. No single fragment of that behavior, removed from its context, reveals any rational purpose.

When by chance, or in an experiment, an animal's instinctive act is interrupted, it is unable simply to continue again from where it left off. It must begin all over again, from the beginning. A frequently cited example is the behavior of the ichneumon fly when it is interrupted while providing for its spawn. The fly drags a paralyzed caterpillar to a previously prepared hole in the ground in order to lay an egg on the creature. But before the fly drags the captured caterpillar into the hole it slips into it itself, as if to see once more whether or not everything is in good order. If this interval is used to move the caterpillar a short distance away from the edge of the hole, the fly acts as follows: It returns to the place where it left the caterpillar, does not find it there, discovers it after a short search, and drags it back to the edge of the hole. It might be expected that the caterpillar would then be stowed away without more ado, since the hole had already been "inspected." However, the fly again obeys the dictates of instinct by slipping into the hole. It will repeat this senseless performance a second and third time, and, in fact, as many times as the experimenter chooses to move the caterpillar away from the hole when the fly disappears into it.

Instinct demands that if one says "a" one must also say "b," and "b" cannot be said at all unless "a" has already been spoken. Instinctive behavior forms are strong and inflexible.

CHAPTER 27

CHILD PSYCHOLOGY

A child's mental life is at first characterized largely by qualitative aspects of his activities. Quantitative aspects play an ever increasing role as he develops. Gradually *"and*-connections" displace the form qualities.

In more concrete terms, the various experiences which fill the child's days imbue its hours with a richly toned quality. For an adult, hemmed in by duties, the day passes quantitatively, by the clock. In particular, the adult's scientific observation retains very little of the child's richly toned experience sequences. Time flows neutrally and homogeneously for the researcher.

The world offers itself to a child physiognomically and expressively, laden with feeling. To a considerable extent the adult in his scientific endeavors can free himself from emotional ties. This accomplishment signifies a qualitative impoverishment of more inclusive wholes. Only with great difficulty can the concept of an abstract number be separated from its concrete attachment to a group form consisting of a number of objects. At one stage of development a child can count his own fingers, but not those of another individual. He has not yet grasped the fact that a number is a quantitative concept which can be transferred from one object to another.

An eminent contemporary linguistics scholar, Jakobson (1940), has made a notable contribution to knowledge of the child's language development. His study emphasizes the holistic approach. Previously it was assumed that a child learned to speak in accordance with the principle of least effort. This meant that the first speech sounds he produced would be those his speech organs could most easily make. For this reason it was supposed that he would employ the easier consonants instead of the more difficult palatal sounds. More recent and more precise analysis of lalling has made that theory untenable.

At the height of the lallation phase a child can produce every conceivable sound and has a repertoire of articulation exceeding the requirements of any living language. It is a remarkable fact that in the transition from lalling to first true speech most of the sounds of the lallation phase drop out again. It is especially noteworthy that even those lalling sounds are lost which are part of the environmental language and which the child must tediously relearn later on. This holds true for palatal and liquid sounds, and consonants as well.

The phonetically rich lalling phase is followed by the first true speech phase with its phonetic impoverishment, in the course of which random lalling is transformed into permanent speech values. The manner in which these initial speech elements are acquired can now be described with some accuracy.

On the threshold of the first speech phase vocalization begins with open vowels; consonants begin with explosive sounds produced in the front of the mouth. Invariably the first vowel is "a" and ordinarily the first consonant is an explosive "b" or "p." This leads to the formation of "baba" or "papa." The first combination of contrasting consonants involves oral and nasal sounds, as in "papa-mama." There follows a combination of contrasting labial and dental sounds: "papa-tata" and "mama-nana." These two combinations constitute the minimal number of consonant sounds needed; they are found in every language.

After the development of consonants just described, there follows the first combination of contrasting vowels. An open and a closed vowel are joined as in "papa-pipi." The next stage may bring a division of the closed vowel into palatal and velar sounds such as "papa-pipi-pupu," or a third intermediate degree of openness, namely "papa-pipi-pepe." Each of these three processes leads to a system of three vowels, which is the minimum number of such sounds in the world's living languages.

Jakobson advances an explanation of the principles governing the development of children's language. He rejects any attempt to explain it on an atomistic basis of single sounds. Organized language does not depend on single sounds, but on the relationship of each single sound to all the other sounds included in it. The successive stages of the child's phonetic development are revealed as meaningful and orderly only in the light of holism. Their progress is in accord with the basic principle of maximal contrast, and proceeds from the simple and unstructured to the graded and differentiated.

The next finding to be discussed is a challenge to any psychology based on elements. It is the fact that the size of an object is not estimated more exactly when it is geometrically simple and has few individual characteristics, but when its form is more fully developed and it has many individual characteristics. In this sense a circle has an advantage over a straight line, and a sphere is judged more accurately than a circle.

The adult, too, judges complex forms more accurately. But the proportionate difference required by an adult is considerably greater than that needed by young children, particularly in estimating everyday objects. A child can detect a smaller difference between two spheres than between two circles. The child's ability to differentiate among spheres of various sizes is more acute than that of adults. Clearly this unusual capacity on the part of the child consists of comprehending and mastering complex wholes rather than elements. It is interesting to add that children are more affected by some optical illusions than is the case with adults.

An instructive experiment can be performed by presenting children with one colored form as a sample and an assortment of other forms, some of which resemble the sample in shape and

Figure 30

others in color. In Figure 30 the triangle to the left of the line is the sample and black represents the color red. Note that the other forms are either white triangles or red squares.

As a rule younger children choose a form of similar color, rather than similar shape, to match the sample. Hence they select a red square to match the red triangle. In reporting this finding for the first time a number of years ago, the writer sought to explain it on the basis of the stronger coherence of identically colored forms (Katz, 1913, page 84). It could also be explained from the standpoint of Gestalt theory by pointing out that color is more important than shape in the creation of forms.

Color, rather than shape, is more closely related to emotion, at least as far as the shapes in Figure 27 are concerned. This fact would suffice to make color more significant for children. It is noteworthy that when adults are presented with the same matching problem, but with tachistoscopic exposure, they follow the children's example and choose a similar object on the basis of similar color. This finding confirms the primacy of color in creating form.

Figure 31

Another experimental procedure for children is illustrated by Figure 31. A sample form is shown in the circle. The child is asked to match the sample by selecting from an assortment of

other forms. But in one instance the correct element is part of a
rigid form, as shown at the left of the circle. In the other instance it is part of an *"and*-summation," as shown to the right
of the circle.

Children find it more difficult to discover the sought-for element in the rigid form. They find the problem more difficult
than do adults. In general the whole has a more binding effect
on its parts for younger children than for older children, and
this influence is stronger for them than it is for adults. The
result is not inconsistent with the fact that children experience
wholes in a comparatively unstructured manner. A child cannot
master the complex structure of a work of art. Its fine points are
apparent only to the connoisseur with his knowledge of the
history of art and his trained aesthetic taste.

As a general principle it may be stated that the more primitive a form is, the more closely it will be tied up with emotion.
Volkelt (1925) writes that the primitive mind has an organizing capacity which, in the case of the adult civilized human,
reveals itself in the tendency to think objectively and in an
orderly fashion. What was characteristic of primitive man
applies to the thought processes of the civilized child.

If a child is shown Figure 32a as a model and is asked to
draw it from memory, the result is shown in Figure 32b. It can

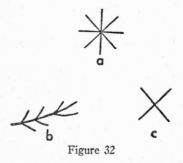

Figure 32

hardly be referred to as a copy. The child transforms the model
in a completely unexpected way. As Volkelt points out, he
thinks of the star-like figure as the branch of a fir tree. A drawing of that kind is produced by an attitude in which emotion
plays a definite part.

When asked whether 32b or 32c resembles 32a most closely, children choose 32b more often, while adults show a preference for 32c.

One of the writer's students * carried out an experiment in which she made use of the optical illusion illustrated in Figure 33. First she placed one segment directly on top of the other to

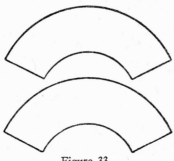

Figure 33

show that they were equal. Then she returned them to the positions shown in the drawing, re-establishing the illusion that one is smaller. The crucial part of the procedure involved the sound of a metronome, an instrument with which the children were unfamiliar and which could be heard when the experimenter moved the segments apart. The children combined the two unusual occurrences and explained them as magically produced cause and effect. A child's consciousness unites two vivid events which occur simultaneously, making them into a single entity. It is a primitive structuring trend. The adult realizes that the two events have nothing to do with each other, and that they really constitute a mere "*and*-connection." The child does not achieve such understanding.

Volkelt adds that what is meaningful and intellectual, on the one hand, and emotional and volitional, on the other hand, have not been sharply differentiated in the primitive wholes of a child's consciousness. Development progresses from the holistic to the aggregative-additive. This characterization of immature mental life also holds true for primitive man.

* K. Raspe.

CHAPTER 28

SOCIAL PSYCHOLOGY

Primitive man thought of the world in terms of magic. For him, all existence was governed by one general principle. The bonds which tied all events together were most firmly drawn.

The primitive mind does not distinguish between reality, dreams, and play. Emotions—above all, fear—obliterate the boundaries between the various strata of mental processes.

What occurs when the more mature mind of civilized man erects partitions between mental strata, as his analytical efforts put an end to the magical interpretation of the world? The result can be expressed in the terminology of Gestalt psychology. The human being who has reached mental maturity displaces inclusive complexes which are rooted in emotion. For these he substitutes objective facts which are connected with each other in a more aggregative manner. For a world image characterized by its qualitative richness he substitutes a world which is comprehended in terms of quantity and is, therefore, calculable. In reality it is his analytical thinking which creates an atomistic world image, and it is this same analytical thinking which tends to rob the world of meaningful qualities and finds quantity alone sufficient. On a primitive level human beings believed they understood a great deal which seems inexplicable to civilized man.

No doubt there are certain "strong" forms in the social life of civilized man. A good marriage is one example. A renowned football team is another. The same can be said of a submarine crew. Surgeon and nurse can be so attuned to each other that they act like one individual with four hands. But the strong forms created by civilized life either have a limited scope, as in marriage, or arise because of technical requirements, as illustrated by the football team. They are not deeply rooted.

There is a marked contrast between the strength of civilized forms and those of primitive man. Levy-Brühl (1923) indicated that commonly held ideas rule the primitive group to such an extent that they completely control its individual members. The community does not depend on individuals. On the contrary, the individual exists only by virtue of his participation in the community. Even birth and death are hardly individual matters, but the concern of the all-embracing social group. The birth of a child enriches the group and the group considers itself weakened by the death of a member. The rise of civilization was accompanied by a loosening of social bonds and a consequent emancipation of the individual. It meant the disintegration of social forms. The speed of this process has been increased constantly by modern technical methods, with their tendencies to break down activities into smaller segments. Society has been atomized to an ever greater extent.

Wertheimer (1925) has contributed to understanding of primitive thinking in a way which emphasizes its qualitative rather than its quantitative nature. He pointed out that contemporary thinking expresses itself in the statement that "All things are measurable. All things are interrelated in an 'and-combination.' " Our numbers are transferable to all sorts of situations. For primitive man, number concepts were by no means transferable in this manner. That is why some groups had more than one system of numerical terms which were used to count various categories of objects. Primitive man attached much more importance to practical, biological considerations. Consider the attitude of one Indian in a mission school. He refused to translate this sentence: "Today the white man killed six bears." He said the story was obviously untrue.

CHAPTER 29

THE PAST AND FUTURE OF GESTALT PSYCHOLOGY

In this concluding chapter it is appropriate to review the question raised in the introduction: Will Gestalt psychology reach a synthesis with the older psychology, as Hegel's formulation suggested?

The question might be rephrased to read: Does the older psychology really offer nothing whatsoever that could be useful for the future?

Whoever answers in the affirmative is abandoning a large amount of psychological knowledge without the slightest justification. Verifiable knowledge may be found in every area of the older psychology, facts which remain facts no matter whether the approach to them is atomistic or holistic. An outstanding example is knowledge of sensory characteristics. Findings in the field of color impressions, as far as the color materials are concerned, have nothing to do with form. The same holds true for the characteristics of the various material agencies that produce sound, smell, and taste. Gestalt psychology is not indifferent to this aspect of the older psychology, as is clearly demonstrated by its interest in the unity of the senses. The new theoretical structure of Gestalt psychology assumed the validity of many facts established by the older psychology.

Gestalt psychologists have rejected the reproach that they did not show enough understanding of the analytic method. They maintained that they had thoroughly analyzed the dependence of form structure on its constituent forms. Their stand was correct, but analysis of the sort referred to does not seem sufficient.

It is completely legitimate to investigate the response produced by stimulation of single sense organs; this was a characteristic interest of the older discipline. It can be expressed without forgetting for one moment that a response of that kind is an artificial product. The mode of response can throw light on many problems of sensory psychology. To state that the older procedure studied an artificial product is an accusation which could easily be reversed and directed against Gestalt psychology itself. Wertheimer's (1912) phi-phenomenon is an artificial product, but it brought welcome insight into functions of the central nervous system.

There is no need to abandon the analytic method employed by the older psychology in its study of perception. The method remains valuable even if many of its findings should be regarded in a new light because of Gestalt theory.

It must be conceded that a system of psychology based on reflexes is open to considerable criticism. However, such criticism by no means implies a ban on the investigation of reflexes. The reflex concept will always render at least some service to psychology and philosophy, even if it is not of prime importance. The pupillary reflex, for instance, is almost completely mechanical. In the future Gestalt psychology must devote some attention to understanding such semiautomatic aspects of the body, whether or not they are reflex in nature.

According to Köhler peripheral arrangement of the visual field is retained up to the *aria striata;* beyond that, he asserted, the process of dynamic self-structuring begins. That is an hypothesis. Its validity can be determined only by analytic study of those visual mechanisms which are actually present.

On occasion the older psychology, oriented toward sensation, was reproached for giving too little weight to higher mental functions which were less closely connected with the senses. In this respect Gestalt psychology itself, so strongly influenced by the problem of perception, is hardly better off. Consider the manner in which Gestalt psychology would describe the mental life of Helen Keller. Visual and acoustic forms do not exist for her. If one can speak of olfactory and taste forms at all, they could not be the basis of mental life. In Helen Keller's case access to the mind was through the sense of touch, but this was not achieved by means of original touch forms. Complexes of touch sensations from raised letters acquired symbolic values for her. Her astonishing development began with the acquisition of these symbols. But what is a symbol as seen by Gestalt psychology? Isomorphism fails to supply an answer.

Gestalt psychology has thrown new light on memory, with respect to both association and recall of images. Yet it is obvious that the altered theoretical viewpoint does not destroy the value of classical memory research. Its findings include such data as the relationship between amount of material and learning time, the effect of repetition, various associative and recall inhibitions, the significance of imagery type with respect to learning method and success in learning, as well as the difference between extent of learning and extent of recognition. These findings belong to the older psychology's stock in trade, and must be reexamined from the viewpoint of Gestalt psychology. But there is no reason whatsoever for abandoning them as worthless.

One of Gestalt psychology's greatest achievements was to point out that the older psychology exaggerated the effect of individual experience and overlooked form-building factors which made such experience possible in the first place. Actually, Gestalt psychologists have no desire to deny the influence of experience. Yet the manner in which Gestalt theorists reject the exaggerations of the older viewpoint might lead the reader to conclude that experience was of no importance. That would be a great fallacy.

All the associations with which the older psychology dealt were not haphazard according to Gestalt terminology, although it is true that the majority were. All the symbols of human speech are haphazard. The form, color, and mode of functioning of almost all objects created by human hands are random; their recognition and handling depend on individual experience. Almost all our forms of social intercourse and social arrangements, knowledge of which is indispensable for good social relationships, may be termed random. If one ruled out all bodies of knowledge, all capacities, and all skills which could be described as having random form, there would be little left for psychology to study.

One of the older psychology's favorite research fields was the investigation of individual differences. It reaches its fullest expression in typology. So many different modes of reaction were discovered, and it seemed so clear that they could not be traced to differences in experience, that psychologists felt compelled to attribute them to innate structural differences. The extent and significance of this branch of psychology become apparent when it is realized that intelligence testing alone, an immense area in its own right, constitutes only one aspect of the differential field.

What is Gestalt psychology's attitude toward differential psychology? To date it has paid little attention to the matter. Elmgren (1939) was justified in raising the question of how Gestalt theory can explain individual differences. To choose an example at random, how can innate asonia be reconciled with the assumption of general dynamic self-regulation of the acoustic field? It is to be hoped that the future will reveal Gestalt psychology's approach to such problems.

BIBLIOGRAPHY

BENUSSI, V. 1914. Gesetze der inadäquaten Gestaltauffassung. *Archiv für die gesamte Psychologie*, 1914, 32, 396–419.

BETHE, A., and FISCHER, E. 1931. Die Anpassungsfähigkeit (Plastizität) des Nervensystems. *Handbuch der normalen und pathologischen Physiologie.* Berlin: Verlag Julius Springer.

CANNON, W. B. 1939. *The wisdom of the body.* New York: W. W. Norton & Co.

DUNCKER, K. 1935. *Zur Psychologie des produktiven Denkens.* Berlin: Verlag Julius Springer.

EHRENFELS, CHR. VON. 1890. Über Gestaltqualitäten. *Vierteljahresschrift für Philosophie*, 1890, 14, 249–292.

ELMGREN, J. 1939. Gestalt psychology: A survey and some contributions. *Göteborgs Högskolas Arsskrift*, 1938, 44, 299.

ERISMANN, T. 1924. *Die Eigenart des Geistigen.* Leipzig: Quelle & Meyer.

FRINGS, G. 1914. Über den Einfluss der Komplexbildung auf die effektuelle und generative Hemmung. *Archiv für die gesamte Psychologie*, 1914, 30.

GELB, A. 1937. Zur medizinischen Psychologie und philosophischen Anthropologie. *Acta Psychologica*, 1937, 193–271.

GOLDSTEIN, K. 1934. *Der Aufbau des Organismus.* The Hague: Martinus Nijhoff.

HELMHOLTZ, H. VON. 1910–1911. *Handbuch der physiologischen Optik*, 3rd ed. Hamburg: L. Voss.

HERING, E. 1905. *Grundzüge zur Lehre vom Lichtsinn.* Leipzig: W. Engelmann.

HUSSERL, E. 1900–1901. *Logische Untersuchungen.* Halle: M. Niemeyer.

ISSERLIN, M. 1910. Über den Ablauf einfacher willkürlicher Bewegungen. *Psychologische Arbeiten*, 1910, 6, 1–195.

JAKOBSON, R. 1940–1942. Kindersprache, Aphasie und Lautgesetze. *Verhandlungen der sprachwissenschaftlichen Gesellschaft in Uppsala.* 1–83.

KAILA, E. 1935. *Personlighetens psychologi.* (*The Psychology of Personality.*) Stockholm: Natur o. Kultur.

KATZ, D. 1911. Die Erscheinungsweisen der Farben und ihre Beeinflussung durch die individuelle Erfahrung. *Zeitschrift für Psychologie und Physiologie der Sinnesorgane*, 1911, 7, xviii and 425.

1921. *Zur Psychologie des Amputierten und seiner Prothese.* Leipzig: J. A. Barth.

1925. *Der Aufbau der Tastwelt.* Leipzig: J. A. Barth.

1932. *Hunger und Appetit: Untersuchungen zur medizinischen Psychologie.* Leipzig: J. A. Barth.

1935. *The world of color.* London: Kegan Paul, Trench, Trubner & Co.

1936. *Conversations with children.* London: Kegan Paul, Trench, Trubner & Co.

1937. *Animals and men.* London: Longmans, Green, Ltd.

1943. Gestaltgesetze des Körpererlebnisses. *Acta Paediatrica,* 1943, **30,** 389–405.

1946. (with Künnapas, T.) Propriozeptiver Reflex und Willenshandlung. *Acta Paediatrica,* **33,** 1–12.

1946. Über Gestaltgesetze geistiger Art. In *Festschrift für John Landquist.* Lund: C. W. K. Gleerups.

1948. The scriptochronograph. *Quarterly Journal of Experimental Psychology,* 1948, **1,** 53–56.

1949. Blendungsphänomene und konnektive Hemmung bei Denkprozessen. In *Nyman Festschrift,* Lund: C. W. K. Gleerups.

KELLER, H. H. and TAKEMASA, T. 1933. Farben im Wechsel-Umfeld, *Zeitschrift für Psychologie,* 1933, 129.

KLAGES, L. 1935. *Grundlegung der Wissenschaft vom Ausdruck,* 5th ed. Leipzig: J. A. Barth.

KOFFKA, K. 1935. Principles of gestalt psychology. New York: Harcourt, Brace & Co., Inc.

KÖHLER, W. 1913. Psychologische Beiträge zur Phonetik. *Katzenstein's Archiv für experimentelle und klinische Phonetik,* 1913, **1,** 11–26.

1920. *Die physischen Gestalten in Ruhe und im stationären Zustand.* Erlangen: Philosphische Akademie.

1933. *Psychologische Probleme.* Berlin: Verlag Julius Springer.

KRAEPELIN, E. 1902. Die Arbeitskurve. *Wundt-Festschrift.* Leipzig.

KRIES, J. VON. 1894. Über die Natur gewisser mit den psychischen Vorgängen verknüpfter Gehirnzustände. *Zeitschrift für Psychologie,* 1894, **8,** 1–33.

KRUEGER, F. 1920. *Das Wesen der Gefühle.* Leipzig: Akademische Verlagsgesellschaft.

LÄPPLE, E. 1942. Eine neue vereinfachte Durchführung zur Auswertung des Arbeitsversuchs. *Zeitschrift für angewandte Psychologie,* 1942, **2.**

LEVY-BRÜHL, L. 1923. *Primitive mentality.* London: George Allen & Unwin, Ltd.

LEWIN, K. 1936. *Principles of topological psychology.* New York: McGraw-Hill Book Co., Inc.

LOEB, J. 1901. *Comparative physiology of the brain and comparative psychology.* London: J. Murray.

MACH, E. 1911. *Die Analyse der Empfindungen.* 6th ed. Jena: Carl Fischer.

MACLEOD, R. B. 1947. The phenomenological approach to social psychology. *Psychological Review,* 1947, **54.**

MAGNUS, R. 1924. *Körperstellung.* Berlin: Verlag Julius Springer.

MATTHAEI, R. 1929. Das Gestaltproblem. *Ergebnisse der Physiologie,* 1929, 1–82.

MICHOTTE, A. 1946. *La perception de la causalité.* Louvain: Inst. Sup. de Philosophie.

MÜLLER, G. E. 1896. Zur Psychophysik der Gesichtsempfindungen. *Zeitschrift für Psychologie,* 1896, **10,** 1–82; 321–412.

1911–1917. *Zur Analyse der Gedächtnistätigkeit und des Vorstellungsverlaufs.* Leipzig: J. A. Barth.

1923. *Komplextheorie und Gestaltpsychologie.* Göttingen: Vandenhoeck und Ruprecht.

MÜLLER, J. 1852. *Elements of human physiology.* New York: Leavitt.

NAGEL, F. 1912. Experimentelle Untersuchungen über Grundfragen der Assoziationslehre. *Archiv für die gesamte Psychologie*, 1912, 23.

PAULI, R. 1943. *Der Arbeitsversuch als charakterologisches Prüfverfahren.* Leipzig: J. A. Barth.

PEDERSEN, R. H. 1943. *Untersuchungen über die Handschrift.* Copenhagen: Munksgaard.

PETERMANN, B. 1929. *Die Wertheimer-Koffka-Köhlersche Gestalttheorie.* Leipzig: J. A. Barth.

PIAGET, J. 1948. *Psychologie der Intelligenz.* Zürich: Rascher.

PLESSNER, H. 1923. *Die Stufen des Organischen und der Mensch.* Berlin: Walter De Gruyter & Co.

RÉVÉSZ, G. 1938. *Die Formenwelt des Tastsinnes.* The Hague: Martinus Nijhoff.

RUBIN, E. 1921. *Visuell wahrgenommene Figuren.* Copenhagen: Gyldendal, Nordisk.

SANDER, F. 1926. Optische Täuschungen und Psychologie. *Neue Psychologische Studien*, 1926, 1, 159–167.

SCHEERER, M. 1931. *Die Lehre von der Gestalt.* Berlin and Leipzig: Walter De Gruyter & Co.

SCHELER, M. 1926. *Wesen und Formen der Sympathie.* Bonn: F. Cohen.

SHERRINGTON, C. S. 1947. *The integrative action of the nervous system.* New Haven: Yale University Press.

SKRAMLIK, E. VON. 1937. *Psychophysiologie der Tastsinne.* Leipzig: Akademische Verlagsgesellschaft.

STERN, W. 1935. *Allgemeine Psychologie auf personalistischer Grundlage.* The Hague: Martinus Nijhoff.

STÖRRING, G. C. 1931. Über den ersten reinen Fall eines Menschen mit völligem isolierten Verlust der Merkfähigkeit. *Archiv für die gesamte Psychologie*, 1931, 81, 257–384.

SZÉKELY, L. 1945. Zur Psychologie des geistigen Schaffens. *Schweitzer Zeitschrift für Psychologie*, 1945, 4, 110–124; 332–347.

VOLKELT, H. 1925. *Fortschritte der experimentellen Kinderpsychologie.* Jena: Carl Fischer.

WACHHOLDER, K. 1925. Beiträge zur Physiologie der willkürlichen Bewegung. *Pflüger's Archiv für die gesamte Physiologie*, 1925, 209; 218–247.

ZEIGARNIK, B. 1927. Über das Behalten von erledigten und unerledigten Handlungen. *Psychologische Forschung*, 1927, 9, 1–85.

AUTHOR INDEX

SUBJECT INDEX